PATRIOTS AND BALLARDS AT GALLOWS
VANDE MATARAM SAGA

PATRIOTS AND BALLARDS AT GALLOWS

Vande Mataram Saga

DR. VINOD SINGHAL

KALPAZ PUBLICATIONS
DELHI-110052

Patriots and Ballards at Gallows : Vande Mataram Saga

Rs. 495

ISBN: 81-7835-560-4

Published in 2007 in India by
Kalpaz Publications
C-30, Satyawati Nagar,
Delhi-110052
Phones : 9212729499
E-mail: kalpaz@hotmail.com

Laser Type Setting by: Rudra Computer Graphics, Delhi
Printed at : Salasar Imaging System, Delhi

At the dawn of the sixtieth year of independence, India finds herself on the threshold of global success. This book is

DEDICATED

TO THE INDIAN RESURGENCE

Contents

1

Introduction

It was a chance encounter; I still remember the date — it was January 26, 2001. On that day, I had encountered an article in a Hindi daily newspaper, written by Sailesh Matiyani, an eminent writer. The title of the article was *Change this National Anthem,* where the writer had condemned the National Anthem *Jana Gana Mana* and lambasted the political masters for not changing it. I was shocked to read such a commentary on our Anthem.

I, a sixty-six years old ordinary run-of-the-mill mediocre medical practitioner, who has to slog daily, even on public holidays, could never claim any time as my own. Life was in a fast-forward mode, and each day passed in a blur. In these circumstances it was futile to even contemplate writing a book, especially when not a world, except medical prescriptions, was ever written by me for the last forty years. But somehow the article by Mr. Sailesh Matiyani stirred me from inside, and I made an effort to obtain all the information I could get on our National Anthem. The more I learned the more intrigued I became. The search took me to Delhi, for there was the National Archives which had valuable information on the proceedings of our Constituent Assembly. The search took me to Kolkata and Shantiniketan, which were the abode of Gurudev Rabindranath. The search took me to Vale of Health, Central London, for here the poet had stayed in 1912. The search took me to Bristol, where Raja Ram Mohun Roy rests eternally. The search took me to the British Library at London, which was a treasure-trove of information in the form of microfilmed newspapers dating back to circa 1911. During my search I met many to seek their views on our National Anthem, and visited innumerable websites to get a clearer picture of the events related to the pre-independence history of India.

Books have always been my best friends, and in the course of my search I came into contact with many, each giving me a thoroughly enjoyable company and such sensuous pleasures which only true friends are capable of giving. Though each one of them was good, but three of them influenced me most. The treatise *India from Curzon to Nehru and After* by Durga Das is a monumental work, which gives first hand and frontline account of the historical events as they unfolded, usually away from the public glare. *Rabindranath Tagore: The Myriad-Minded Man* by Krishna Dutta and Andrew Robinson, a superb painstakingly done research work, presents Tagore in a true light, unlike most of the others which generally are mere compilations of folklores. Last, but not the least, is the voluminous history book *Raj: The Making and Unmaking of British India* by Lawrence James, a British professor of history, who with the help of documents recently released, has candidly narrated the history of the British occupation.

Eventually the information convinced me that injustice had indeed been done to Vande Mataram, and unwarranted honours were bestowed upon Jana Gana Mana. It was then decided to present the factual information found in the form of a book, which is in your hands.

It took me five years to collect the information, and one more to write the book. While every care has been taken to check and double check the facts, it is possible that some inaccuracies may have crept in it.

While penning the book, for days, I found it impossible to be critical of Gurudev Rabindranath and Pt. Jawaharlal, the two worthy sons of India, for they have my great respect. Then one day it occurred to me that everyone in the universe admires the eternal brilliance of the sun, and its brilliance was not diminished when Galileo, a few centuries ago, discovered black "sun spots" over the solar surface. Tagore and Nehru are two suns over the Indian horizon, and their shine will remain as it ever was, whether a few blemishes are described or not.

Frequently I found it difficult to continue with the writing, but each time it was either the words of encouragement from my wife — she is no more — or the inspiration from Vande Mataram which kept me going. For decades the mantra, that is Vande Mataram, has inspired the ordinary people to do the extraordinary, and its power is still as potent as ever.

Prof. Brij Mohan Gupta regards himself fortunate to have been a disciple of the legendary Dr. Puttulal Shukla, an eminent authority on Hindi poetry. I am grateful to him for elucidating the finer points of *Saar Chanda*, and helping me with the analysis of the metre of Jana Gana Mana by providing a rare book *Adhunik Hindi Kavya mey Chanda Yojna* by Dr. Shukla.

I am indeed indebted to Mrs. Gurbaksh Kaur and Prof. Asif Hussain, my friends, who read the manuscript with care and offered me valuable suggestions. The favour extended by Mrs. Gurbaksh was commendable, as it involved reading the manuscript scribbled in a doctor's handwriting, which at times was nothing better than the markings left by an ink-soaked insect crawling on a paper. Mr. Asif not only professes English but is a walking repository of Urdu couplets. It was he who provided me with the beautiful couplet on paper-cartridge by Bahadur Shah Zafar, the poet Emperor of India.

I shall forever be obliged to the courteous staff of The British Library, St. Pancras, British Library Newspapers, Colindale and National Archives of India, New Delhi, for their valuable and prompt help. I am also thankful to The Friends of Arnos Vale Cemetery, Bristol, for showing me around the burial ground and providing the literature related to it.

2

Beginning of the End

The Might of a Cartridge

The rifle was British, the bullet that came out of it was British, and the target it found was also British, but the index finger that had pulled the trigger was that of an Indian. His name was Mangal Pandey, a sepoy of the 34th Native Infantry, then stationed at Barrakpore, a town in Bengal Presidency.

When the Commanding Officer of the Presidency division, General Hearsey, got Mangal Pandey arrested on that fateful day of March 29, 1857; little did he realise that he was witnessing the beginning of the end of the British East India Company, whose paid employee he was. Mangal was court-martialled and the all-white-court, at the end of a week long trial, awarded the expected death sentence. By sending Pandey to the gallows, the authorities wished to end the episode. Even the Governor-General Lord Canning and his advisors at Calcutta, only seventeen miles away from Barrakpore, thought so. Actually they were all witness to the beginning of the most destructive storm that was ever encountered by the British East India Company in its entire 257-year-long existence.

The storm had been gathering its destructive power for quite sometime, from a seemingly small cartridge of the recently introduced Lee Enfield rifle. All over the world, armies had long ago discarded the guns called muskets, and were adopting ever changing and innovative models of rifles. Those who missed the change, lost almost every battle fought with plain muskets against rifles. While the guns were effective only up to twenty yards, a rifle on the other hand could, with ease, pick a target five hundred feet away. Soldiers with muskets had strict orders to commence firing only when they could see the white of their enemies' eyes, which is generally seen from a distance of fifty feet.

The uncanny accuracy of the rifle was due to the spiral grooves on the inside of the barrel which imparted a spin to the bullet, when it moved out after being fired. It was a slow gyroscopic movement, about one complete spin during the ten to fifteen feet flight of the bullet in the air. The spin enormously increased the accuracy and the firing range of the rifle which in the mid-19th century was still loaded from the muzzle, the front end of the rifle. To load a rifle, first a measured quantity of gunpowder, then a cotton wad and after that a lead ball, were all rammed down the muzzle, separately, with the help of an iron rod, one after another. In the end a small quantity of cotton was again pushed to hold the lead ball in place which otherwise could roll out of a tilted rifle. After each shot, the barrel was thoroughly cleaned; for gunpowder of those days left considerable residue. This long and tedious process involved as many as thirty steps. Understandably, even a trained sepoy could fire only three shots in one minute.

To increase the firing power of its army, the East India Company introduced the newly developed Lee Enfield rifle and a paper cartridge, containing gun powder charge, cotton wad and a lead ball, all in one envelope. In a single step, all could be rammed down the muzzle, but only after the cartridge was activated by biting off, by teeth, the marked end of the envelope containing gunpowder charge. It was also possible to tear off the marked end by hands, but it required both hands and forced the sepoys to place the rifle on the ground, to be picked up again, only after the envelope was torn and one hand was free. This manouevre considerably increased the loading time and was never put into practice. The sepoys were required, by order, to bite off the paper cartridge. To facilitate the ramming, the paper envelope was heavily greased with lard — a mixture of animal fats. While biting, a quantity of lard always remained in the mouth. Since cow and pig fat was cheap, it was purchased from the local bazaars and used. This cheap fat turned out to be very expensive. It was responsible for the ultimate downfall of the British East India Company and the cost was, its 'Raj of India.'

Too Few Win too Many

It was the last month of the last year of the 16th century and London was as usual, freezing cold. The gaiety of Christmas was over and people were once again free to attend to the mundane chores of life.

On the command of their Queen, two hundred and eighty merchants, knights and other nobles gathered in a hall, to ponder over Britain's worsening financial condition. By this time many European powers had established trading links with Eastern countries, significantly and constantly adding to their prosperity. Britain was lagging behind.

Traditionally, Britain always was and remained a nation importing agricultural products to feed her ever growing population. The cost, especially of tea and spices was prohibitive, but to keep her subjects happy, the Queen had to perpetually import these commodities. To trade directly and gain access to the east and far-east markets, she proposed a trading company, and it was for this purpose that the wealthy of Britain had assembled. The financial resources of Britain, at that time were so dismal that even the 218 richest men of Britain could only muster a kitty of seventy thousand pounds. In other words, on an average, each noble was rich enough to contribute a petty sum of three hundred and twenty pounds only, that too, under the command of their own Queen. A company was formed and on December 31, 1600, the Queen of Britain, Elizabeth I presented the royal charter to this company, giving it the exclusive rights to trade in the east for a period of fifteen years. At that time there were many other companies trading in the east and to differentiate this company, it was popularly called the British East India Company.

During and before the rule of Elizabeth I of the Tudor dynasty, England was regarded by other European nations, as an uncultured and a barbaric country, who was always quarrelling and stealing from her civilized and rich neighbours because she was never able to produce enough to feed her hungry millions. Britain had not much to export; and import of food could only be made by paying in gold and silver, which were slowly disappearing from her treasury. Hunger made Britain a nation of looters. Her sailors became pirates, and these predators were set loose on the high seas, where they would follow their prey, which generally was a galleon returning to her home-port after a trading trip. These British pirates stalked their unsuspecting prey, and attacked at the appropriate opportunity. After looting all that was of any value, pirates slaughtered every living soul found on that ill-fated ship, so that no one was left to disclose their horrid tale. To destroy the last remaining witness to their crime, the ship was set on fire. No clue of piracy was ever left to disclose their deeds.

The most celebrated of all, was pirate Francis Drake, who was privately chartered by the Queen of England, Elizabeth I, to loot. This sea dacoit brought such great riches to the treasury of Britain that this spinster Queen, herself used to go to the harbour to receive the returning ship of pirate Drake. He eventually was knighted by the Queen and the pirate Drake became Sir Francis Drake.

Another pirate, near and dear to Queen Elizabeth was Walter Raleigh. To keep him near, the spinster Queen had appointed him the captain of the Queen's Guard. He too was knighted, but when his secret marriage to an English beauty was detected, in a jealous rage, Elizabeth got him imprisoned in the Tower of London. He was released when the royal rage subsided. The next ruler of England was a male, who could not be as kind to him as the spinster Queen was. He sentenced Raleigh to death, on repeated complaints of piracy.

The grateful nation still remembers her pirates. A life size, fully dressed bronze statue of pirate Raleigh, with an unsheathed rapier in hand, proudly stands in the front courtyard of the Greenwich Institute of London.

A nation can never be fed forever on the riches of loot alone. At the most, it can only be a temporary affair. Elizabeth knew it and to fill this gap she gave a charter to the East India Company.

Unlike the Dutch; Britain did not have a planned and effective maritime strategy. As a result, initially, the East India Company failed to achieve the desired objectives and had to feel satisfied with what ever remnants of trade were left over from the Dutch East India Company strongholds. It could only establish its first trading post, eleven years after the charter was presented, at Machlipatanam in India in the year 1611. The Queen died two and a half years after the East India Company came into existence and started its activities. Because of the opposition from her ministers, the Queen could not marry the hero of her dreams, the King of pirates Sir Frances Drake and died unmarried. Her end was bitter, for she died without a Tudor claimant to the Royal Crown or a thriving East India Company, her pet creation.

For the next one and a half centuries the existence of the Company was devoid of any excitement and depended entirely on the pleasure of the local native rulers of India. The working of the Company was so lacklustre and mediocre that many humorously nicknamed it 'John Company'. The Company also behaved well and confined its activities to commercial trading only. The Company imported textiles, cotton, calicoes, muslins, indigo, black pepper and other spices from India. These products were paid for in silver which Britain had earned by trading with Europe and America. This is how—by trading with Britain and other nations— India became, and even today is, the largest reservoir of silver in the world; though not a gram of it was ever commercially produced in the country. From India such a huge quantity of quality textiles was imported that in 1719 the English weavers cried:

Every jilt of the town
Gets a calico gown;
Our own manufactures are out of fashion[1].

Slowly the East India Company prospered. In 1744, it even loaned one million pounds to the British Crown. By now it had about 2000 shareholders, and was paying regular yearly dividends of 8 to 10 per cent.

By the middle of the 18th century the political scenario in India was in a flux. On account of the peculiar historical events, the central dominant power of India was in the hands of Muslims, who were in a distinct minority and believed in a religion that was fundamentally different from the faith of the Hindus, who were in an overwhelming majority.

Although Muslims for several centuries were the rulers of a large part of the Indian territory, they were always apprehensive of the Hindu majority and developed a minority complex. The population of India at that time was about

180 million, out of which only 17 million were Muslims and the rest were, almost all Hindus. The proportion of Muslims, in the earlier centuries was even less and the ruling class was like an island of Muslim minority, surrounded by a vast sea of the Hindu majority, and this created a deep sense of insecurity in the minds of the ruling Muslims, who did their best to keep Hindus financially and militarily weak by imposing taxes like Jazia and by prohibiting the possession of arms. Although many of them had the foresight to treat Hindus with respect, and offered them key posts in the royal court, but a few bigots committed atrocities, and lost the Hindu sympathy and cooperation. The result was disasters, and the once invincible Mughal army was reduced to a pathetic state.

India was ready to be won by almost any military power that could defeat these inept rulers. White men in battalion strength, with rifles in hand and following modern war tactics, started defeating, with ease, armies thirty times bigger. Men like Clive and Wellesley came to India and won territory after territory with only a handful of English soldiers. In the Battle of Plassey, Clive defeated the 50,000 strong army of the Muslim ruler of Bengal, Sirajuddaula, with only 800 (eight hundred) white-soldiers and 1500 native sepoys. Eight hundred overpowered fifty thousand. Too few won too many.

3

War of Independence

End of the East India Company

India never allowed rustics to remain rustic for long. There was something in her air, which soon mellowed all of them. Alexander the Great came and here his greatness was lost. The Mighty Mughals came and soon their might too was lost. Now it was the turn of the wily white men. The land of plenty had made them complacent; the dazzle of riches made them blind and the Indian prosperity made them wishful day dreamers. Robert Clive in a letter to his home had described Murshidabad—the capital city of Bengal province— as about the same as London in population and size and that the only difference was, its inhabitants were more prosperous. At that time Murshidabad was just one of the many main cities of India. Most of them were even richer. General David Ochterlony, the company resident at Delhi from 1803 to 1825, smoked a hookah, watched nautch-girls and had a harem of thirteen native concubines[2]. It was usual for English officers of the company to have a personal staff of 5 to 6 servants to attend to their needs. The adopted lifestyle of the English in India made them soft.

The incident at Barrakpore was taken lightly. Even Lord Canning, the British Governor General of India, did not pay much attention to the incident, though he was in Calcutta and only 17 miles away from Barrakpore. No serious efforts were made to analyse the behaviour of Mangal Pandey. Cow and pig eating Englishmen knew precious little about the religious psyche of the Indians.

Sepoys, by traditional method, used to take no less than twenty seconds to load all the components, one by one, into the muzzle of the rifle, before firing. A trained sepoy could charge the same rifle, with the integrated paper cartridge, in ten seconds flat and, fire six rounds in one minute, which was unheard of, so far. The lure of doubling the fire power of their army, without adding a single sepoy to the pay-roll, blinded the East India Company officials. They continued to press for the use of the greased cartridge.

Barely a month and a half after the Barrakpore episode, the 3rd light cavalry at Meerut also refused to use the obnoxious cartridges and with their refusal, the British C-in-C went berserk. For this minor offence he got all the native sepoys arrested. Their number was eighty-five. An all white court-martial sentenced them to ten years of rigorous imprisonment. In front of the whole garrison, at an appalling ceremony, the sepoys were humiliated, uniforms torn; legs shackled with iron bars and hands tied with iron chains. Then all were dragged like animals to their prison cells, where ten years of hell awaited them.

White men staged the highly provocative and inflammatory act in the presence of the three regiments of Indian sepoys, who under order were made to witness the cruelty meted out to their friends. If the white men had wished to install a feeling of awe, fear and submission, they failed miserably. If their intention was to provoke and make the Indian sepoys angry, they not only succeeded but succeeded beyond the limits of their imagination. Each and every sepoy was fiercely angry, but that anger was still not enough to breach the army discipline. For it, a little more provocation was needed, and that came on the very next day, which was a Sunday, the Lord's Day, regarded holy by all Christians. That fateful Sunday was May 10, 1857 and on that day Christian white- men disobeyed the order of their Lord. It was His fourth of the Ten Commandments, which had directed them to—

> "Remember the Sabbath day, to keep it holy".
> (IV Commandment)

White men made that Sabbath day unholy. They tortured the Indian sepoys in their prison cells. It was the force of the shrieks of the tortured, which breached the army discipline. War was declared against the tyranny of the English and by evening forty white men were dead. The Lord had punished those sinners, who had disobeyed Him.

The war of independence soon spread to the many other regions of India, specially Delhi and Oudh. The war of 1857 was fought by the Indians, with the aim of destroying the English Company and to end its despotic rule. The war achieved that aim and the notorious 257-year-old East India Company was totally and permanently wiped off from the Indian sub-continent.

The insignificant paper cartridge played a significant role in the war of independence. The last Mughal Emperor Bhadur Shah is credited with the couplet:

> Iran ne kiya, na Shahenshah-e-Roos ne,
> Angrez ko tabah kiya Kartoos ne.

(The English, who conquered Persia and defeated the Czar of Russia, had been overthrown in India by a simple cartridge)[3].

The war for independence killed thousands and changed India, which never again was to be the same. It affected the lives of millions, and one of them was Allan Octavian Hume, an Englishmen. The events had taken him by total surprise and without any warning signals. Utterly mystified by the act of the natives, Hume vowed to, one day, solve the riddle of the mysterious Oriental mind. Another of them was Bankim Chandra Chatterjee, a nineteen-year-old Bengali college boy. The sacrifice of his fellow compatriots made an indelible mark on his psyche, and proud Bankim too vowed to glorify the motherland one day.

The war also affected the life of Ganga Dhar Nehru. His ancestors had come to Delhi in 1716, to seek employment in the court of the Mughal Emperor, Farrukh Siyar. Since then, for generations, the Nehrus served in the court of the Mughals, and when the war of 1857 reached Delhi, Ganga Dhar had the plum post of the city Kotwal (head police constable).With the down fall of his impotent Muslim master, Ganga Dhar with his family joined the countless refugees fleeing towards Agra; where even bare survival was an onerous struggle. He lost the struggle when he was not even thirty-five. He would have died in peace had he known that one day his grandson, Jawaharlal Nehru, would return to Delhi, this time not to serve any master, but to rule over India.

4

Birth of Congress

An Attempt to Understand the Mysterious Oriental Man

Before the year 1858 could end, India's war of independence became a part of history and so was the East India Company. But what could not be relegated to history was the nightmarish experience of the war. When the 1857 war began, there were 2,57,000 Indians and only 34,000 European soldiers in the Company army in India. Indians could have overwhelmed the British, if they had wanted to[164]. Many Hindus—most famous of them were Rani Lakshmi Bai and Tantia Tope, who became heroes of the masses —fought the war along with Muslims, but not all of them, and their numbers were significant. Had they not hesitated to fight under the green flag, the white men would have lost not only the East India Company but India as well. It was, once in a lifetime chance for a nation and Sikhs and Hindus seized it to end the tyranny of the Muslim sword. White men were allowed to retain India for a while longer. All though the white men were now the masters of the land, they remained mystified by the behaviour of the oriental men. Many white men attempted to solve the mystery, but failed every time and a frustrated Kipling warned: "You'll never plumb the oriental mind ..." [4] to which Sir Walter Lawrence agreed "No one can boast that he really understands the Indians. The more that is learned about him, the more the student is aware of his ignorance". [5] The fact was, all over India, the white man had made many small Englands, and he lived there, alone. There he had, for his use only, stores, streets and schools. There he not only had his exclusive clubs, but played only European games, and where the native Indians were allowed entry, only as servants. This created a divide without a bridge. At last Rudyard Kipling made a great discovery "East is East and West is West, and never the twain shall meet". [6] And they never, ever met. Anglophiles found it a monumental discovery, elated they presented the Nobel Prize to Kipling in 1907.

Out of the many white men, who had tried to solve the oriental mystery, one was an Englishman, and his name was Allan Octavian Hume. He had joined the Bengal civil Service in 1849 and from Etawah, a small town near Kanpur; he started his service career, and became an assistant commissioner of revenue of the East India Company. Like all other members of his race, he too had no inkling of the impending calamity. When the war of 1857 broke out, he had to flee from Etawah. To save his life, he had to disguise himself. On that day, he vowed, to one day fathom the depth of the oriental mind. His chance came when he was able to convince the Viceroy, Lord Ripon, of the importance of a forum, where leaders of Hindus, Muslims and other communities would meet. There they would be encouraged to bare their intimate thoughts and give the government an opportunity to fathom their mysterious oriental mind. There they would also be allowed to suggest ways and means, by which it would be possible for the British government to mould itself, to be more acceptable to the masses of India. Ripon approved the idea and gave Hume the responsibility to convert it, into a reality.

By now, the pre-1857, despotic rule of the East India Company had been replaced by the British Crown, which was careful enough to project itself as a benevolent regime. Hume proceeded with caution and sugar-coated the concept with lofty ideas. To begin with, he drafted a letter, which was addressed to all the graduates of Calcutta University—the largest educational centre established by the British—and which churned out the most amenable educated minds in the country. The letter dated March 1, 1883, invited all the graduates of the university, to join a forum, called the "Indian National Congress". Challenging their patriotic instincts, he wrote, "if you, the picked men, the most highly educated of the nation, cannot, scoring personal ease and selfish objects, make a resolute struggle to secure greater freedom for yourselves and your country, a more impartial administration, a larger share in the management of your own affairs, then we, your friends, are wrong and our adversaries right; then are Lord Ripon's noble aspirations for your good, fruitless and visionary; then at present at any rate all hopes of progress are at an end, and India truly neither lacks nor deserves any better government than she now enjoys. Whether in case of individuals or nations, self sacrifice and unselfishness are the only unfailing guides to freedom and happiness" [7]

Whether, it was the East India Company or the British crown, Hume's services to the Empire remained uninterrupted and his loyalty above suspicion. Even the blind could have seen through the motives of this Englishman. His love and care for Indian nationalism was that of a wolf, trying to guard a flock of sheep.

In 1884, Lord Dufferin replaced Ripon as the new Viceroy of India. He too approved of the plan. Hume had decided to invite the Governor of Bombay, Lord Reay, to preside over the first session of Congress. Dufferin opposed it and advised him to select a native, to get better cooperation from the Indians. In 1884, Hume went on a tour of the presidency towns of Calcutta, Madras and Bombay, to meet the political leaders of India. There was no need to persuade them. It was sufficient to mention that his plan had the approval of Lord Ripon and the blessings of Lord Dufferin. It was impossible for the so-called leaders of India, not to agree to a plan in which two Viceroys were involved. If there was any misgiving about the proposal, it was never aired in public. The option to doubt the motives of Her Majesty's representative was simply not available to the Indians of that time.

Initially there was a tussle between the Bhadraloks of Calcutta and the Gentlemen of Bombay, as to who should be given the privilege of hosting the first session of Congress. The numerical number and the loyalty of Bengal outweighed any other claim, but if Calcutta was selected, there was every possibility that only a few delegates from Bombay would attend the event. A situation like this would have reduced the first national session to the status of a regional meet.

Bengal and Maharashtra were, more or less, equal in importance to the "Raj," and both were almost always equally treated. To balance the delicate equation, Hume decided to alternate and divide the honours. He selected Poona of Maharashtra as the venue of the first session, to be presided by a Bhadralok from Bengal. Calcutta was to host the next meet for which president ship was reserved for a Maharashtrian Gentleman. In spite of this delicate balancing, everyone from Bengal was not pleased. Surendranath Banerjee was in command of an organisation known as "The Indian Association" whose aim was similar to the proposed Indian Congress. Surendranath not only abstained from the Congress, but organised at about the same time, a national conference of the "Association" at Calcutta. [8] Like all other graduates of Calcutta University, he too had received the Hume's letter, and knew about the Congress session, well before time. The following year he attended the Congress meet, when the venue was Calcutta. Later on, he became a very active and prominent member and eventually the President of the Indian Congress. He was a close friend of Rabindranath Tagore.

Keeping in view the convenience of Europeans and Christians in India, Hume selected a date which was immediately after Christmas. By this time the celebrations of the most important Christian festival were over, and at the same time India was comfortably cool for the Europeans. The tradition to hold the Congress session in the month of December, immediately after Christmas, was religiously followed for almost three decades. By then Indians, in the presence of Gandhi and Tilak, had become bold enough to complain about the bitter cold of Lahore and Allahabad. Dates were then changed according to the comfort of the Indians.

Just before the first Congress session, a few cholera cases were reported from Poona. In India, parasites of malaria and bacterias of cholera had killed a far greater number of the Hume's clan members, than all those killed by swords and bullets. The Europeans were terrified and the venue was shifted to Bombay.

The Congress of that time was open to all, and any Indian or European could join in, as a delegate. All that was required was the payment of the delegate fee of rupees ten, a significant amount in 1885, which is almost equal to Rs 5000 of today. Although, all the proceedings of Congress were conducted in English, the knowledge of it was not mandatory. Many came and went back, without understanding a single word of the proceedings. Emphasis was on pomp and show, and when it was found that even the sum of rupees ten was not sufficient to maintain it, in

1901, the delegate fee was doubled to rupees twenty. Committees of the Congress devoted far more time and energy in the preparation of exotic menus, than in drafting resolutions. A few of the selected fortunate, at times, even managed to tour England, on the pretext of presenting memorandums to the British rulers. Congress delegates were treated with lavish parties by the British governors and Viceroys. While the Governor of Bombay, Lord Reay hosted a treat to the delegates of the first session; it was the Viceroy of India, Lord Dufferin, who offered a superb feast for those, who had come for the second Congress meet at Calcutta.

Allan Octavian was a happy man, when he entered the large hall of Gokuldas Tejpal Sanskrit College on 28th day of December 1885. The Indian Congress, so far only a pipe dream, was at last going to become a reality. It was, exactly at noon, when he called the meeting of 72 delegates to order. The first day of the life of the Indian National Congress had begun, and with it started the uninhibited and shameless show of flattery of the British Royal crown. These tails wagging Congressmen were known as moderates. The Congress of today, officially describes them as "... a class which was Indian in blood and colour, but British in taste, in opinions, in morals and in intellect. They were supporters of British institutions." [9] Moderates were proud of being part of the British Empire and always remained loyal to the British crown. One of the Congress presidents, Dadabhai Naoroji proudly declared: "Let us speak out like men, and proclaim that we are loyal to the backbone, that we understand the benefits, the English rule has conferred upon us" [10] Not to be left behind another Congress president, Surendranath Banerjee, in trying to prove that be was even more loyal, advised Indians: "Let us work with unwavering loyalty to the British connection... It is not severance that we look forward to, but unification, permanent embodiment, as an integral part of that great Empire" [10]. On another occasion he said: "To England we look for guidance...

England is our political guide, our moral preceptor in the exalted sphere of political duty. [10] Moderates were proud to be a part of the British Empire and regarded themselves fortunate to be the subject of that Empire, as was confirmed by one of their presidents, Pandit Bishan Narayan Dhar. Speaking from the dais of the 1911 session of the Congress at Calcutta, he declared: "I thank God, that I am a British subject and feel no hesitation in saying that the Government of India by England.... is still the greatest gift of Providence to my race". [39] They found considered it their sacred duty to serve the British monarchy. To love and give loyal support to the empire was their patriotism. For them, India was an integral part of the British Empire, and India as an independent and sovereign nation, had no place in their thinking.

Moderates were proud of being ruled by the Queen of England. In the Congress sessions, her life size portraits and after her death, of the King, were prominently displayed, along with the Union Jack. The Queen, and after her, the king was lustily cheered.

In the honour of the British King, poems were specially composed and sung. At the Bombay session of 1904, this poem was proudly recited:

Disunion and discord
Are the ruins of India caused,
To restore her then
To her ancient prosperity,
And to develop her
With Britain's help,
Cooperate with your wealth
Industry and enterprise.
That King Edward's glory
May shine throughout the world. [11]

The early Congress was confined to the annual sessions. Between the two sessions, there was almost no activity and the activity at the sessions was limited to "... begging through prayers and petitions," [12] and "the foreign rulers treated them with contempt." [12]

Moderates were sycophants to such an extent that at many sessions they invited the British, to preside over the Congress meet. To prove their loyalty and to flatter the English president, it was a must for all the moderates to register their presence in that particular Congress session, as can be seen by their attendance. [13]

1st Congress session of 1885 Indian president	-Bombay Delegates present 72.
2nd Congress session of 1886 Indian president	-Calcutta Delegates present 406.
3rd Congress session of 1887 Indian president	-Madras Delegates present 607.
4th Congress session of 1888 British president	-Allahabad -George Yule, an industrialist of Calcutta. Delegates present 1248.
5th Congress session of 1889 British president	-Bombay -Willium Wedderburn, an ICS officer of the British Government. Delegates present 1889.
6th Congress session of 1890 Indian president	-Calcutta Delegates present 677.

7th Congress session of 1891	-Nagpur
Indian president	Delegates present 812.
8th Congress session of 1892	-Allahabad
Indian president	Delegates present 625.
9th Congress session of 1893	-Lahore
Indian president	Delegates present 625.
10th Congress session of 1894	-Madras
British president	-Alfred Webb
	Delegates present 1163.

At all these meets of the Congress, the count of the delegates was in hundreds, but whenever there was a white man presiding over the session, the number of delegates was always in thousands.

The cunning genius of an Englishman had invented the institution of Congress, to keep a vigilant eye over the mysterious Oriental man and his equally mysterious mind. Who could have been more suitable than A.O. Hume to manage the institution? Hume had devoted all his life to earn an impeccable reputation, as the faithful of the Empire. He had proved his loyalty, by hanging to death, seven Indians, who were suspected to have taken part in the 1857 war of independence. [163] Still, Hume had the confidence of the Congressmen, to such an extent that he was requested to be the Secretary General of the organisation.

The confidential reports of the Secretary General, on the affairs of the Congress in general, and Indian political leaders in particular, proved to be so valuable that the Empire insisted on his continuance in the same post, for as long as it was possible for him. Hume remained, uninterruptedly, the Secretary General of Indian National

Congress from 1885 to 1906, an unbelievable period of twenty-two years. During this period, presidents changed, and they changed every year, venue changed, and it too changed every year. Delegates changed and the Constitution changed, but the only thing that did not change, year after year, decade after decade, was the General Secretary of the Congress. Every file moved through his desk, every letter passed through his hands and every meeting was conducted in his presence. Diligently he kept sending the detailed report on every event, to the British Empire.

The early Congress consisted entirely of moderates and remained in their complete control since its beginning in 1885 to 1905. For the first time, their authority was challenged in 1906, at the 22nd session of Calcutta. The 1905 partition of Bengal, by the Viceroy, into two parts, one predominantly Hindu and the other Muslim, was strongly resented by all Indians. As a result, a strong wave of nationalism was seen, all over the country. A distinctly separate group emerged within the Congress, and many more from outside joined, to gain a new identity. The members of this group were known as nationalists, but the moderates, the British authorities and the press under their influence, insisted on calling them extremists. According to a reputed Indian historian, the difference between these two was: "The moderates believed in loyalty to the English throne. They also believed that the continuance of British rule was in the interests of the people of India. The view of the extremists was that the British rule in India was a curse and the question of (their) loyalty to the English throne did not arise at all." [14]

At the Calcutta session of 1906, the nationalists made a determined move to gain power in the Congress. A large number of them got registered as delegates and all of them made it a point to remain present, at the crucial time of voting. While in the preceding year (1905) there were only

756 delegates, at Calcutta the number was doubled. There were 1663 registered delegates, and with ease the nationalists outnumbered the moderates, whose loud protests could not stop the nationalists from moving resolution after resolution, censoring British rule. Each one of them was adopted by the house. The main resolutions were:

(i) Demanding reversal of the partition of Bengal.
(ii) Upholding the boycott of British goods.
(iii) Supporting the Swadeshi movement.
(iv) Protesting against the educational policy of the government.
(v) Asking the people to take up national education.
(vi) Demanding self-government for Indians.

For the first time, at the Congress session, a new slogan was heard. It was the slogan of "Swaraj" by Lokmanya Tilak.

The Calcutta session had a profound effect on nationalists, as well as on moderates. Nationalists were naturally elated on their first ever win, and looked forward to, once again, reacting to their performance at the next session, come what may. On the other hand, the moderates were depressed, but certainly not defeated. The Congress always belonged to them and they vowed to keep it with them only. And why not? Hume was with them and, through him; the all powerful British Empire was there to help them.

The next session of the Congress was scheduled to be held at Nagpur, where the reception committee had planned to propose Lokmanya Tilak as the president; a proposal which was unacceptable to the moderates. They prevailed on Hume, the Secretary General, to change the venue to Surat, the port town where three centuries ago, one of the first British ships had anchored to start the trading activities of the East India Company. Moderates believed that three hundred years of British influence had made Surat, once a town, now a city, a safe and secure place for them to stage the next Congress session. Safety was the only reason for the moderates to opt for this coastal city, otherwise Surat at that time was an inconvenient and poorly connected city for an all India gathering like the Congress session. In the over one hundred-year-long history of the Indian Congress, the city was never again selected as the venue.

In spite of the tedious and inconvenient journey to Surat, both the moderates and the nationalists had come in large numbers. They had come fully prepared for any eventuality. When the Congress met on December 27, 1907, the atmosphere was surcharged by many rumours. In a pre-planned move, the moderates proposed the name of Dr. Rash Behari Ghosh, a top - notch leading lawyer from Calcutta. When Surendranth Banerjee rose to say a few words in support of Dr. Rash Behari, the nationalists shouted him down and forwarded the name of Lala Lajpat Rai, and in turn were, counter shouted down by the moderates. The noise made it impossible to conduct any business and the meeting was adjourned. The following day at the meeting, Dr. Rash Behari, in an indecent haste and without following the required procedure, was elected as the president. When Lokmanya Tilak protested from the dais, the moderates tried to suppress him roughly. Shoes were hurled and some people with *lathis* (thick bamboo sticks) in their hands, were seen rushing to the dais. There was a body fight in which blows, *chappals* (sandals) and *lathis* were freely used. Many were seen with blood flowing.

The Surat meet was suspended and the session was declared null and void. The 23rd session was not counted and instead of this, the next session at Madras was recorded as the 23rd session. It is on official record that Surendranath Banerjee was whole heartedly with the moderates. After the Surat fiasco, there was a complete vertical split. The

Congress remained firmly under the control of the moderates, and the nationalists were barred from attending, any meet of the Congress. Tilak, the chief architect of the nationalist movement, was arrested on cooked up charges, on June 24, 1908 from Bombay, and sentenced to six years of imprisonment. He was deported to Mandalay in Burma, a place so for away that none of the nationalists could ever meet him, to take his advice.

As usual, a detailed report of the events was submitted to the British regime, by Hume. As a result, "The British government tried to win over the moderates against the extremists (nationalists). There were frequent meetings between the moderate leaders and the Viceroy. After the Surat split, while the extremists (nationalists) were roughly handled by the government, the moderates were shown all the favours. Lala Lajpat Rai, Sardar Ajit Singh, Tilak and many leaders of Bengal were deported [15]. It is another matter that after the Surat split; the moderates realised their real worth, in the eyes of the public. Their popularity nosedived and the number of delegates at their meets was reduced remarkably. In the very next session there were only 617 delegates, and a year after in 1909, they were reduced to a pitifully low figure of 243, although the venue was Lahore, an all time favourite, and a much respected and famous public figure, Pandit Madan Mohan Malaviya, founder of Benaras Hindu University, was especially invited to be the president of the session.

For eight continuous years after the Surat meet, from 1908 to 1915, the Congress remained firmly in the hands of the moderates, who regarded themselves subjects of the British Empire and not of India. For them, their loyalty was for the King Emperor of Britain and his praise was the height of patriotism.

The First World War forced many changes in the world, and the world of moderates also changed. After a gap of eight years, the nationalists were not only allowed, but were honourably invited to participate in the 1916 Congress session of Lucknow. With the return of the nationalists, the popularity and number of participants also, once again, increased. The Lucknow meet was attended by a record number of 2301 delegates.

5

Golden Years of Calcutta

Calcutta was the Capital of India

When Job Charnock came to Bengal towards the end of the seventeenth century (1690) and selected a tiny fishing village for the British trade settlement, even in his wildest dreams, he had never imagined that one day this village would metamorphose into the capital of British India. What Charnock could not dream of became a reality when Warren Hastings, the first Governor General of India, in 1772, moved all the important offices from Murshidabad to Calcutta. From that day onwards, Calcutta never ceased to add one grandeur after another. It soon became the most affluent and glamorous mega metropolis of the British Empire. By the end of the 19th century there was hardly any luxury in the world that Calcutta did not have. You name it and Calcutta had it, and had it much before any other city in India. Be it the first:

Printing Press (James Hickey-1780)
Newspaper (*The Bengal Gazette* 1781)
Governor's House (1804)
Town Hall (1813)
Vernacular Magazine (*Digdarshan* in Bengali-1818)
University (Calcutta University 1857)

Tram car (Horse-drawn 1873)
Daily Newspaper (*The Statesman* -1875)
Museum (Calcutta Museum-1875)
Sports Association (Indian Football Association 1888)
Electric tram car (1902)

Calcutta was the first city in India to have an international standard hotel — The Great Eastern Hotel. It also had the first high court and first medical college. It could boast of being the first city to have electricity, piped water, piped cooking gas and endless other firsts. It was here that the English were welcomed most. They wrongly built the 'Gateway of India' at Bombay. It should have been at Calcutta because from here they actually entered India, and it was their real gate of entry. It was not that Calcutta got its pomp and prosperity for free, for it was paid for by the miseries and famines of Bengal. If Calcutta was an island of pomp and plenty, Bengal surrounded it by her poverty and pathos. Calcutta was also the epicentre of the activities of the moderates.

In 1911, when the moderates heard that the King Emperor was going to visit India, they were ecstatic. For the moderates the King Emperor was no one else but the real incarnation of the Almighty, and that Almighty was actually going to set foot on their land.

The Indian Congress met to choose the venue for this important session of 1911. Many names were suggested and the most popular one was Delhi. So far this important city, soon to be the capital of India (from 1912), had never been the venue of even a single Congress session , while relatively less important cities of Allahabad and Lahore, had been the venue three times, but the moderates from Calcutta were adamant. Under any circumstances, they did not want this singular opportunity to welcome the King Emperor, passed on to another city. Moreover in no other city, could complete loyalty and reverence to the crown be ensured. The moderates did not want a single word to be uttered form the dais of the Congress, which could be regarded as disloyal to the King. Calcutta was their fort and from that city alone, they could guarantee a truly faithful welcome to the dispenser of India's destiny, King George V of Britain, and so, Calcutta was selected for the sixth time, as the venue of the 1911 session of the Indian Congress. Delhi had to wait for seven more years for its turn to come, and eventually the session of 1918 was held there.

For this prominent event, the Congress decided to invite an Englishman, Ramsay MacDonald, to preside over the 1911 session. He was the same Englishman who later on became the Prime Minister of Great Britain. He, in 1909, was responsible for the introduction of a separate electorate for Muslims. Commenting on the separate electorate for Muslims, one eminent historian writes: "It cannot be denied that the effect of communal representation was the establishment of Pakistan in 1947"[16]. He was also instrumental in the appointment of the controversial Simon Commission. The untimely death of his wife prevented him from becoming the president of this important session, and Pandit Bishan Narayan Dhar, as the last minute choice, became the president of the Congress.

As usual, this session was also full of sycophants, who exploited every available opportunity to exhibit their art of praise, mastered over the years.

Bhupendranath Basu was the chairman of the reception committee. He found the king like God and proclaimed, while speaking on the reunification of Bengal by Royal decree "... It has pleased God, after much suffering and tribulation, to hear our prayers and through His own instrument on earth He has proclaimed the fulfilment of our vow ... Our heart is full to overflowing" [17] Talking about the King, he added: "He is today protected not alone by the bayonets of his soldiers and the loyalty of his Indian people but also by the prayers of millions of his humble but devoted subjects in Bengal. To him we accord our homage and welcome not only as our King and Emperor but as our deliverer"[17]. Mr. Basu crossed all limits of sycophancy when he declared that the welcome for the King was equivalent to the one given to Sri. Ram Chandraji, God of all the Hindus. He said: "... enthusiasm with which we are greeting our King today and for which no parallel exists in the annals of India, unless we travel backwards over the fading footprints of departed time, through the dim vista of a legendary past when Ram Chandra made his triumphal entry into Ayodhya, the ancient capital of the solar race"[17]. Not a single voice of protest was raised by the moderates, against the comparison of a mortal with Shri Ram Chandra, the much worshipped God of Hindus.

The Congress President, later on, disclosed in his speech the significance of a 'Patriot' to the Congress of that time. Speaking on the annulment of the partition of Bengal he said from the Congress dais: "The royal boons not only are a proof of British justice and benevolence, they show that the old order is changing, giving place to some thing new and better, that supreme government is determined to rule us according to its best and noblest traditions, and that if we appeal to it in a just cause and convince it by our persistent and patriotic endeavours that we are earnest and sincere, it will never fail to respond to our appeal"[17]

The use of the word 'patriotic' in this speech clearly reveals its meaning for the Congress. To the Congress, display of loyalty to the British crown and sincerity to the King Emperor were patriotic endeavours.

As was the tradition, the Calcutta session started, a day after Christmas, from December 26, 1911. To show their loyalty and praise the King, the moderates had dedicated the next day of the session, for this purpose. Surendranath Banerjee, an influential member of the Congress and main organiser of the event, had specially invited his close friend, Babu Rabindranath, to inaugurate the day, with his poem 'Jana Gana Mana', which was specially composed by him to welcome and praise the British monarch and his wife.

6

Rabindranath Tagore

He and His Family

In Bengal, Rabindranath Tagore is present almost everywhere, but is still not easily found. He has been installed on a pedestal so high, that he becomes almost invisible from the daily life of Bengal. Nirad Chaudhuri, a prominent writer from Bengal, found Rabindranath "Nothing more than the holy mascot of Bengali provincial vanity".[18] According to folklore, Rabindranath was actively involved in the freedom struggle of India. While every other participant of the struggle was imprisoned for varying periods, Tagore was never, not even for a day, sent to jail. Probably his struggie was so friendly and benign that the need to imprison him was never felt by the British government.

The Brahmin family of Tagore followed an unconventional code of life and path of opportunities. They had migrated to Bengal, probably in 1000 A.D., on the invitation of the Hindu king of that time, and remained with this dynasty for as long as the Hindu kingdom lasted. By the fifteenth century, the rulers of Bengal were Muslims and soon the Tagores became intimate with them, particularly with the Vazir (Minister) of the governor of Jessore— Muhammad Tahir Pir Ali. To cement the intimacy, the Vazir was often invited to dine with the Tagores, who too in due course, were invited to feast with the beef (cow's meat) eating Muslims. The sacrilegious behaviour of the Tagores infuriated the Hindus, who could not overlook their intimacy with the beef eaters. The only punishment available, within the power of the Hindus, at that time of Muslim rule, was out casting of the offender, so the Tagores were out casted from the Hindu community. As the excommunication was for their association with the Vazir Pir Ali, they were henceforth known as the Pirali Brahmins, and barred from marrying high caste Hindus.

When the East India Company came to rule Bengal, the Tagores with their uncanny ability, once again recognised the opportunity and switched their loyalty, and now white men, and not the Muslims, were their friends. An individual member of the Pirali Brahmin clan was called Thakur, a tongue twister for any white man, who found it easier to pronounce it as Tagore. To please the new masters, the family changed its surname and the Thakurs became Tagores. The English were indeed pleased, and involved the Tagores in many of their services. The Tagores collected taxes for the Company, built Maratha Ditch to protect Calcutta from frequent Maratha raids and supervised the renovation of Fort William at Calcutta.

The Tagores flourished and soon amassed a small fortune, as the middlemen, in the trading of the white men. This trade in fact was nothing else but a form of loot of Bengal. Jawaharlal Nehru commented: "It was pure loot... this process was called trade...but that made little difference...This so-called trade was plunder" [19]

Rabindranath's great great grandfather, Nilmoni Tagore had served directly under Robert Clive, after his victory in the Battle of Plassey and made plenty of money.

The Tagores were now rich and they built a palatial mansion at Pathuriaghat, a river side prospering town of Bengal.

Money is the root cause of many problems, and for money, there was a rift in the Tagore family. Nilmoni left Pathuriaghat with his share of money and reached Calcutta, where he built a big house at Jorasanko. One day, in a room of this house, Rabindranath was born, and 80 years later died in another room of the same house.

Both branches of Tagores—Pathuriaghat and Jorasanko—soon learned the secret of the success. They discovered that plenty of wealth was available at the pleasure of the whiteman and nothing pleased them more than flattery. Both branches were to perfect and make it a fine art. They mixed their natural talents with sycophancy, added a dash of luck and garnished with the cooperation of fellow Bengalis. The concoction thus prepared was then coloured bright with loyalty to the British crown, which proved to be potent enough to make the Tagores one of the wealthiest and most prominent families of Bengal.

Sorindermohan, a Pathuriaghat Tagore, was a naturally talented musician. He adeptly mixed his talent with a huge portion of sycophancy and out came 'Victoria-Gitika', a flunkey praise of Her most Gracious Majesty, Queen Victoria. This was sycophancy of such an order that even the British found it embarrassing and had to defend him by saying: "The generous exaggeration of a loyal poet, especially when the poet is an Oriental, must not be counted a fault"[20].

Twenty-six-year-old Devendranath Tagore formally became a Brahmo on December 21, 1843, and embarked upon a life of contradictions. He was the father of Rabindranath. He called himself a Hindu yet rejected the Hindu way of life to such an extent that he, the eldest son, did not partake in any of his father's funeral rituals. He discarded all the Hindu symbols, yet wore the sacred thread, a mark of high caste Hindu, to the last day of his life. He abhorred all the Hindu customs, yet in 1873 performed a three-day-long Hindu religious ceremony, Upanayan. As a Maha-Rishi he was supposed to shun family life, yet he fathered no less than fifteen children. Brahmo Samaj commands its followers to always speak the truth, yet he suppressed the truth. In 1884, when his daughter-in-law Kadambari committed suicide, he bribed the press to suppress it[33].

By the time Rabindranath was born in 1861, the Jorasanko Tagores had built a formidable 125 years long impeccable record of loyalty to the white rulers of India. As Rabindranath grew up, attempts were made to educate him. Though, as many as four different schools were tried, he failed to fit into any one of them, and whatever could be taught to him was taught at home. Years kept on adding, but no one noticed in the crowded household — he had fourteen siblings, their wives and children, his parents and several other relatives — that he was only partially educated. One day he became a man, and a search was mounted to find a suitable bride for him. Though decades had passed, but the stigma of being a Pirali Brahmin was still there, and no high caste Hindu was prepared to marry his daughter to him. Though there were good looking and educated Pirali maidens, but somehow they were not interested. Unable to find a good looking bride for Rabindranath, the family started to search for any girl. At last they found in Jessore town, now in Bangladesh, a Pirali girl, and her name was Bhabatarini. She was illiterate, not good looking and only ten years old, and her father was a poor employee of the Tagores. He agreed to marry off his daughter to Rabindranath. On December 9, 1883, twenty-two-year old Rabindranath married a girl who was not even half his age.

The child became a mother before she could celebrate her thirteenth birthday, and next year, she was again pregnant. The immature tree was repeatedly made to bear fruit. Bhabatarini died at the tender age of 29. The fruits too were weak, and out of her five children, three died young.

In 1887, Rabindranath delivered a forceful lecture, in which he appealed to his fellow countrymen to abandon child marriage, but he married off one of his daughters at the age of ten and a half and the other, at thirteen.

It was a well-established British policy to encourage the show of loyalty in her Indian subjects and sycophancy was accepted as a form of loyalty. For his show of loyalty, Pathuriaghat Tagore, Sorindermohan was awarded a doctorate in music by Oxford University and thus, in 1896, he became the first Indian to receive an honorary doctorate from Oxford. This University could not find another suitable Indian to confer a doctorate for the next forty-four years. Whoever was proposed was either not talented or loyal enough to receive the honours.

After 44 years, it was the time for yet another great war. The Second World War had started with bad news for Britain. Her armies were routed at every front in Europe, and Great Britain was never as helpless as she was in the days of May and June of 1940. Her defeated and tired 3, 35,000 strong army, trapped by German Panzer divisions, on the sandy beaches of Dunkirk, was desperate to cross the English Channel, which separated it from the relative safety of Britain. The arrogant British Empire was on her knees, looking for support and help from every possible corner of her territory. At that time, Lord Irwin, a former Viceroy of British India, was the Chancellor of Oxford University. He was well aware of Tagore's influence and his magical hold over the masses. He knew that by honouring Rabindranath, support and help from the whole of Bengal could be easily ensured, so he proposed the name of Tagore for a doctorate and Oxford University, which in the past had rejected his name[21], agreed to confer the doctorate on Tagore. He at that time was in India, and because of the fierce battle at sea, it was not safe for him to personally go to Oxford, but such were the compulsions of the war for the British Empire that the University was made to take the unprecedented step of going, all the way, to Tagore's doorsteps. The last soldier of the retreating, British army was evacuated from Dunkirk on June 2, 1940. Soon after that, the name of Rabindranath was proposed for the doctorate, and, in record time, was accepted by the University. A special Oxford team was assembled, and with this team the doctorate scroll crossed the war time sea, on a risky journey. To reach Shantiniketan from Dunkirk, the Empire took only 65 days, and on August 7, 1940, a Jorasanko Tagore became the second Indian to get the honours. He is the first and the only one in the history to receive the Oxford degree, from the comforts of his own private drawing room.

On that day, Rabindranath said: "... I accept this recognition from Oxford University, as a happy augury of an age to come, and though I shall not live to see it established, let me welcome this friendly gesture as a promise of better days". Any one who was a friend of Tagore was the friend of Bengal as well. The Tagore influence, once again worked, and the British Empire did not face any serious trouble in Bengal, during the period of war.

Many other Pathuriaghat Tagores also excelled in showing their loyalty to the Empire. One Pathuriaghat Tagore became an Indian member of the council of the lieutenant governor of Bengal.[22] Another one of them was created, by the British Empire, a Maharaja in 1877, after the Queen Her Highness Victoria assumed the title of 'Empress of India'. He was also honoured by the British government as the head of a family "... conspicuous for loyalty to the British government". Another Pathuriaghat Tagore was selected by Lord Curzon to represent Bengal at the coronation of Edward VII.[23] Needless to say, that the loyalty of the Pathuriaghat clan made them one of the most powerful and wealthy families of Bengal.

The Jorasanko Tagores were not far behind from their Pathuriaghat cousins. Rabindranath's grandfather, Dwarkanath Tagore, was remembered most for his colourful life. He loved making money and money of any hue, even the one earned by 'smuggling opium'[24] was welcomed. With his money he lived such a lavish life that in Calcutta he was known as a 'Prince'. He liked the title so much so, that he insisted on being called 'Prince Dwarkanath'. To entertain his white masters, Prince Dwarkanath even built one European style Villa at Belgatchia in Calcutta, where he earned a distinction, rare for a native Bengali, who could invite the Governor General for dinner, and actually sit at the table to dine along with him.

7

Raja Rammohun Roy

A willing Victim

From time to time, the English devised many plans to consolidate their colonial rule of India. Raja Rammohun Roy was a victim of one such plan. He, a high caste Brahmin by birth, is generally known as the founder of the Brahmo Samaj and exponent for the abolition of Sati, an appalling and unfortunate Indian custom. He became very rich while he was in the service of the East India Company and did trading for it. Rabindranath described Raja Rammohun as "the best friend of my grandfather". There were quite a few similarities in these two best friends, as both loved money and earned a lot of it under the patronage of the East India Company. While one of them was a king (Raja) and the other a prince, they both died in England, the country they loved most.

Rammohun Roy, a great linguist, had hold over many languages and mastery of English. He was also a great intellectual, but had pawned his intelligence with the English by collaborating to bring Christianity through the Hindu backdoor in the disguise of the Brahmo Samaj. Members of the Brahmo Samaj were called Brahmo Samaji or simply Brahmo, after the name of the Hindu God Brahma, the God of creation and writer of the voluminous epic the Mahabharata. He is one of the three— Brahma, Vishnu, and Mahesh— forms of God, but unlike the other two, he is rarely worshipped. Out of estimated 35 lack temples of various Gods and Goddess in India, Brahma has only one temple, at Pushkar, dedicated to him, where he can be worshipped, if one wants to.

Any movement that could weaken the Hindus was encouraged by the English, and for this reason only the Brahmo Samaj was lionised by them. They had correctly presumed that by alienating the Hindus from their dharma, the Hindu way of life, more loyalty to the British Raj could be expected; making the rule of the white men easy and lasting.

On November 19, 1830, when Raja Rammohun sailed to England, he was a very rich man, and after four and a half months of sea voyage when he landed at Liverpool on April 8, 1831, he had complete confidence in his business agility. So far Rammohun had been phenomenally successful in the business, and now in Britain he hoped to impress the English with his business ability, which was an illusion made possible by the patronage of the East India Company. In Britain he was on his own, and without the support of the East India Company he started losing money. Before he could realise his true business worth it was too late, and he failed to honour many of his business commitments, for which he was dragged to several courts of law for cheating. The lawyers' fee and court's expenses were so many and so high that he soon became a pauper. At this crucial time not only his friends but even his own family, believing him to be a cheat, deserted Rammohun, and he had to depend on charity, even for his daily food.

Dejected and rejected, Raja was no longer a Raja. Forced to live a recluse's life in poor and unhygienic conditions, he soon fell ill with meningitis—an infection of the brain. Rammohun, born as a high caste Hindu, when died on 27th September of the year 1833, was no longer a Hindu, either in belief or in practice, and respecting his wishes his body was not cremated. As there was no one prepared to bear the expenses of a cemetery funeral, his body was buried in the free land at the backyard of the 'Beech house' of Stapleton at Bristol, where he breathed his last.

For the next decade he remained forgotten, and no one noticed the indecent burial and the unwept demise of Rammohun. After the long period of ten years, when the East India Company was in search of an acceptable loyal native, who could be projected as a great Indian in the books of the newly opened schools and colleges of the Company, he was again remembered, and his name was retrieved from the dusty basement of oblivion. The title of Raja, given to him by the politically impotent Muslim ruler of Delhi, Akbar II, was never recognised by the East India Company. This title, ten years after his death, was not only remembered again but made official. Moreover one more honorary title of 'Bahadoor' was added to his name, and he was now known as 'Raja Rammohun Roy Bahadoor'.

Rammohaun, now touted as one of the greatest ever born on the subcontinent of India, overnight became a hero of the British East India Company. In 1843, an emissary from Calcutta was specially deputed by the Company, after providing considerable funds, to exhume the decade-old dead body of Rammohun. His mortal remains were once again buried, this time in a proper coffin, at the expensive Arnos Vale Cemetery in the same Bristol town, where his dead body previously remained buried in an unmarked grave for ten years.

With the advent of the 19th century, plunder from India had made many in Britain wealthy, and these wealthy men demanded to be buried in style after their death. A few enterprising businessmen recognised the potential, and a privately owned joint stock company, Bristol General Cemetery Company, with profit as the aim, was floated in the year 1837. This company was the owner, as it is even today, of the Arnos Vale Cemetery, situated on lush green landscaped 45 acres of rolling land at the outskirts of Bristol city.

According to the law of the land, no one was allowed to bury the dead in a consecrated cemetery, without the rites of the Church of England. Arnos Vale was a consecrated Anglican cemetery, and there was no place in it for those who were not Christians. Even those Christians were denied burial who did not follow the rites of the Church of England, and for these dissenters a separate seven acres of land, separated by a sunken fence, was set aside. Rules were so strict that even Christian husband and wife were not allowed to be buried side by side, if they both did not belong to the Church of England. It is on official record that Mary Matthews, wife of a wealthy and influential resident of Bristol, was denied burial next to the grave of her husband. While her husband was an Anglican, she was not. She was buried a little away in the seven-acre plot, separated from her husband by a sunken fence.

On a very expensive front portion of the Anglican section of the cemetery, a sculptured tomb of Rammohun was erected, where he was buried after the mandatory rites of the Church of England. Designed by William Princep, the tomb is made of solid Bath Stones, and even today, out of all the graves, his is the biggest and most massive. The East India Company must have spent a fortune on it.

The tomb was shaded by a specially acquired exotic flowering tree. Today, the tree and Rammohun's ideas have both wilted and stopped flowering. The tomb is shaped like a Hindu temple, with temple like pillars and a temple like canopy, there is even a temple like pinnacle. But in the centre there is a tablet, which declares that he endeavoured 'to suppress idolatry and... tended to advance the glory of God.'

Picture of tablet (By the Author)

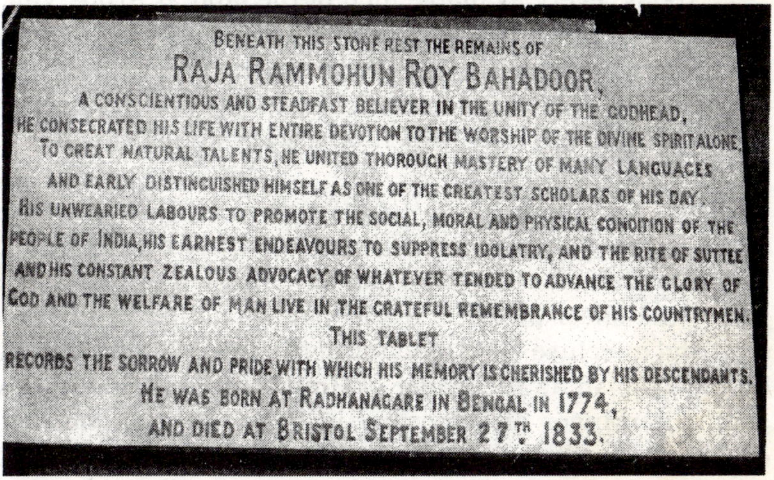

What a similarity the tomb had with its master, who long ago died along with his ideas, and was now lying inside it. The tomb only looks like a Hindu temple, but it actually is a Christian grave in an Anglican cemetery. Rammohun looked a Hindu, complete with a Hindu dress and a Hindu *pugree* (head gear), but inside him he cherished Christian ideas.

Arnos Vale cemetery had ample facilities for cremation. According to the official records of the cemetery, so far 7,50,000 dead bodies have been cremated, compared to only 250 thousand, which have been buried. Clearly a vast majority had quietly adopted a Hindu custom by opting for cremation, which definitely is a superior way to treat the dead. In cremation, every trace of infection is eliminated by the purifying flames of fire, leaving the living community safe from the spread of deadly diseases; moreover it occupies very little precious land. The dead never encroach the land of the living; from where once they go, they go forever. These arguments were obviously not for Rammohun, for he abhorred all that was Hindu and had his body buried.

Today, every available inch of the land at Arnos Vale has been occupied by the dead. With no more land to sell, the owners announced, in 1998, the permanent closure of the cemetery. The dead had once again occupied 45 acres of precious urban land which otherwise would have been used by the living.

The man — who was accused of forgery and cheating in the British courts, who could save himself from certain jail by the sheer power of his money, who died as a failed man and a recluse, who renounced Hinduism — was touted by the English as the leader of Hindus, a great son of the soil, a harbinger of modernity in India, because he had collaborated with them in the anti-Hindu campaigns. Seeing the truth through the haze of lies, Mahatma Gandhi called Rammohun Roy a "pygmy"[27] intellectual.

The name and the so-called fame of Rammohun Roy are mostly attributed to his campaign against a horrific Hindu ritual known as *Sati* (Suttee) or widow burning, a custom to be loathed by all at all times. In the British House of Commons, hundreds of hours and thousands of pages were devoted to the consideration of *Sati*. The British were excessively obsessed with this Hindu custom. As early as 1815, in India the British Raj started to police *Sati* in order to discourage the practice. In 1829 Lord Bentinck, Governor General of India, banned *Sati* by an order, about which the government was never serious in implementing. Barbara T. Gates, a professor at the University of Delaware of U.S.A says: "The surprising thing about this particular British obsession was that Suttee, though appalling to the Westerners then as now, was neither so prevalent nor as widespread as the British attention to it would suggest. From 1817 to 1827 there were some four thousand Suttees in a population of over 160 million, and most of those were localised to Bengal—Calcutta in particular"[28]. *Sati* was a kind of suicide and many more than this number committed suicide in Europe, then or at present. Even the founder of the British Raj in India, Robert Clive, committed suicide.

C.A. Bayly speculates that "Nineteenth century concern over Suttee was intensive because, beginning in about 1820, feeling against Hinduism ran high and Suttee was the most blatantly barbaric custom that could be used in an anti-Hindu campaign"[29]. Starting from the 13th centaury and ending in the 18th, there is a little talked about chapter of European History, known as the Witch Hunt era. Though the entire continent was affected, its impact was felt most in Germany, France, Italy and Switzerland, where its fury was at the peak from 1550 to 1650. During this period tens of thousand — according to some European historians, about 9 million — females were executed, generally by burning at stakes. The aim, by pointing out this custom, is not to condone the ritual of Sati — which could never be justified, as it was an atrocious and awful act — but to point out the fact that while English were accusing Hindus for *Sati,* their own people were burning innocent women, and the number was much more. In the small territory of Scotland alone, about 1500 were executed[174]. True, one wrong cannot justify another, but it does expose the English intention, which was less to help Hindus to give up this horrendous custom and more to malign them. The huge hue and cry made by them for *sati* was missing when the equally barbaric Witch Hunt executions were taken up for discussion.

To loot India, it was essential to rule India, and India could be ruled from democratic Britain, only by moulding the opinion of the vote giving British public against Indians in general, and Hindus in particular. Rulers from Britain wanted to paint Hindus black, and they could not find any colour blacker than Sati. Raja Rammohun provided a convenient handle for the brush with which the Hindus were painted black. During that period, *Sati* was also practised in countries other than India, but these were never criticised the way India was. Edward Westermarch, a Finn who taught at the London school of Economics towards the end of the 19th century, observed "... in spite of imperial prohibitions, sutteeism of widowed wives and brides has continued to flourish in China down to this day and meets with the same public applause as ever"[30]. In Japan suicide, known as hara-kiri, till only a few years ago was regarded as an honourable act. In ancient India, *Sati* was not practised. Most probably this deplorable custom was adopted during the unprecedented upheavals of the medieval times when a large number of males died, in recurrent wars and skirmishes, and left behind a considerable female population, for which there was no one to provide for in a society, which somehow had to cope up with its meagre resources. Perhaps, at that time a need for a practice like *Sati* was felt and adopted by the Indian society, as the Witch Hunt was by the Europeans, to deal with the redundant female population.

Before the second half of the 18th century could end, the East India Company had become a monster out of control, and powerful enough to play havoc, both in India and England. It was an empire within an empire, and the empire of the Company in many respects was bigger than that of the British Empire. The total strength of the Company's army was more than the British army. The territory under its control was bigger than England. A far greater number of people paid taxes to the Company than they were paying to the British government. The Company was answerable to no one, while the British government was to the parliament.

News that Clive had secured the entire revenue of the rich and affluent Bengal started a boom, and the price of the East India Company shares sky rocketed. For almost ten years, the East India Company shares remained the favourite of the Bulls, and ruled the London stock exchange by its might. By 1767, the Company shares were at its all time high. The bubble burst with the report of the attack of Haider Ali on Karnataka, and the once favourite share of Bulls was badly mauled by the Bears. The infamous 'Bengal famine' of 1769-70, caused by the gross misrule of the Company and claiming millions of human lives, made the Bears at the London stock exchange, even more active. By 1770 the finances of the East India Company were so bad that its almost entire balance sheet was splashed with red ink. The once provider, begged for financial help from the British government.

In 1766, the East India Company had agreed to make an annual payment of 4,00,000 pounds to the British government, headed by Lord Chatham, the Prime Minister, in lieu of assistance rendered to it by the government army and a small garrison of British crown troops, that supplemented the vast Company army in India. It was a small sum and the Company always promptly paid it, but by 1770, the finances of the Company were so deplorable that even this small sum was not paid. In fact in January 1773, it had to take a loan of one million pounds, from the Bank of England.

Loans, dwindling share prices and tales of misrule tarnished the image of the East India Company and its officials, were generally regarded by the voting population of England as "brutal blood suckers" and guilty of "rapine and oppression"[31] in Bengal. This was also the conclusion reached by the Commons' Select Committee chaired by General John Burgoyne.[31]

Against this indictment, the East India Company maintained the view that it was justified in perpetuating despotic rule in India because Indians had become accustomed to misrule. The British government did not wholly agree with the Company view, and in 1773 passed the 'Judicature Act', which made the Supreme Court possible at Calcutta. Almost at the same time there was a very strong attack on Robert Clive in the British Parliament which he survived, but with a severely tarnished reputation. As a result in England there is not a single public statue of Clive, or a street, or a park, or a square named after him. He now tried to soothe his nerves by regularly taking opium, but without any lasting solace. The end of opium-addicted Clive was as ghastly as his career was. Disgraced, at the relatively youthful young age of 49, he committed suicide by slitting his throat with a razor blade.

The suicide of Robert Clive could not pacify the public, and it continued to bitterly criticise the Company and its officials. In May 1782, the Commons of the British Parliament demanded the "dismissal of the Governor General of Bengal, Warren Hastings, on the ground that he acted in a manner repugnant to the honour and policy of the British nation".[32] The House of Commons argued for two years for stringent regulations for the East India Company, and in the end, the India Act of 1784 was passed which placed the territories of the Company under the Board of Control, whose president was a member of the Cabinet, answerable to the Parliament. Warren Hastings was impeached in the spring of 1786, but before the final order could be signed, the case dragged on further for nine more years. In the end, the might and resources of the Company saved Hastings, and he got an acquittal.

Financially ruined and under repeated attacks in Parliament, the East India Company was in search of ways and means by which it could save its reputation. The Company surmised that if India could be projected as a nation inhabited by barbarians, it could justify the harsh and unjust methods adopted by it, to rule them. Hindus formed 85 per cent of the population, and if they could be associated with *Sati*—such was the image of *Sati* in the psyche of Britain—then the whole of India could be proved to be inhabited by barbarians. However, there was a big road block in the way. The reputation of the East India Company directors and officials was such that no one in Britain would have believed them, no matter what they said. To be successful in achieving their goal the Company needed a reputable native Indian, and Rammohun was that person. He was intelligent, knowledgeable, articulate and spoke English very well. Above all he was, by birth, a high caste Hindu. Rammohun fell into the cunning trap of the East India Company which used him to tarnish the image of the Hindus. This "pygmy intellectual" was the prime factor in perpetuating the Hindu shame which they never deserved. No Hindu scripture has ever advocated Satism, and even in the Hindu *Mahabharata*—the most voluminous epic ever written in the world, recording millions of deaths in wars, duels and otherwise, as a result of which thousands of women became widows—not a single incident of *Sati* is mentioned in any of its several volumes.

Rammohun or no Rammohun, the custom of Sati would have fizzled-out, had a few more years been allowed to elapse.

8

Making of Jana Gana Mana

A Song of Slaves

In 1911 Rabindranath was over fifty, but he, still, did not have any achievement which could be called worthwhile. The school Shantiniketan, founded by him, had not earned a good reputation. There was even a government circular which found Shantiniketan 'altogether unsuitable for the education of the sons of government servants'[35]. Tagore had written a few books in Bengali but the education department officials of Bengal had rejected all of them for schools, as his writings were not found up to the expected mark [35]. The Bhadraloks of Bengal had not liked his satirical play *Achalayatan* and there was even resentment over his novel *Gora*. He had inherited wealth, but along with it was attached the stigma of being a sympathiser of the foreign rulers. He was still a poet known only to a few, and was addressed by the title of Babu. At that time in Bengal, anyone who dressed well and had some knowledge of English, was called Babu.

When it was known that King Emperor George V and his wife, Queen Mary of Teck, were scheduled to visit India and be coronated at Delhi, loyalists of the British Empire were jubilant. A national reception committee was constituted to make arrangements to welcome the royal couple. Surendranath Banerjee also was a member of the reception committee. All the sympathisers and loyalists of the Empire were eager to participate in the ceremonies associated with the royal visit and the coronation of the King, but only a few were successful. The Pathuriaghat Tagores were among those who succeeded, and they were permitted to hold a ceremonial parasol over the royal head, while the King sat on the silver coronation throne.[36] To hold the parasol was a footman's job, but the head of the Pathuriaghat Tagore felt greatly honoured by it.

The Jorasanko Tagores were those, who could not get a chance to show their loyalty to the British King. Rabindranath had specially composed a song, Jana Gana Mana, with the hope to recite it on the occasion of the coronation, and it was submitted for approval, to the national reception committee. Surendranath was a member of the committee and he strongly recommended the song by praising it as a patriotic song of a loyal subject of His Majesty, the King George V. However, there was a serious flaw, and the song, in spite of the efforts of Surendranath, was rejected.

Dutta and Robinson, after researching on the subjects for more than ten years, found "Most probably it (song Jana Gana Mana) was really composed for the occasion of George V's coronation at the Durbar held in Delhi in the same month (December 1911)—but not sung at the Durbar because it was insufficiently 'Loyal'. There the head of the Pathuriaghat Tagores held an umbrella over King George; perhaps the Bengalis on the national reception committee had hoped that Rabindranath could manage a song in the same spirit as the umbrella. If so, they were disappointed.[35] Rabindranath was disappointed but was consoled by his friends. No doubt, a Pathuriaghat Tagore was able to show his loyalty, by holding the umbrella and the Tagore from Jorasanko was denied. But all was not lost, and there was still another chance to show his loyalty. Surendranath promised him an opportunity, to sing the song at the Congress session, scheduled to be held at Calcutta, a few days after the coronation Durbar. Surendranath was one of the organisers of the Calcutta session, and an invitation was sent to Rabindranath to present his song there.

On Wednesday, December 27, 1911, the second day of the session started at 12 noon. Though the gates were open an hour before the proceedings started, many of the delegates were still absent. Rabindranath was first on the list and without waiting for more delegates to arrive, he was asked to present his song. After reciting his song, Rabindranath left the venue without submitting the customary copy of the song. The official record of the Congress for 27th Dec'1911 reads "The proceedings commenced with a patriotic poem composed by Babu Rabindranath Tagore".[37] No details of the song were given.[38]

There were several English and vernacular newspapers which reported the proceeding of the Congress meet. Only one of them, *The Bengalee*, found the song 'patriotic'. It wrote: "The proceedings commenced with a patriotic song composed by Babu Rabindranath Tagore, the leading poet of Bengal *(Jana gano mano adinayak)* of which we give an English translation".[40]

Translation of the Song, as published in *The Bengalee*

1. King of the heart of nations, Lord of our country's gate,—Scinde, Guzerat, Maharasthra and the Punjab, Dravida, Utkala and Bengal, the Vindyas and the Himalayas and the heaving waters of the Jamuna and the Ganges—they waken at thy name, they crave thy blessing, (together) they raise the hymn of thy praise. Dispenser of all good to nations, king of our country's fate—we salute thee, hail all hail to thy name.

2. Thy call, it spreads, day and night. The Hindu, the Bhuddhist and the Shiks, Jains, Parsees, Musalmans and Christians—East and West—thy large utterance has brought them together to the purlieus of thy throne; and there they stand linked in the bonds of love. Bringer of unity to nations, king of our country's fate—we salute thee, hail, all hail to thy name.
3. Uneven is the road of life, (starred) with rise and alternate fall; and down it, through the long process of years, have trod, the sons of men. On this road, thou art one charioteer, O Lord; the sounds of thy chariot wheels fill it day and night; and thy trumpet rings loud in hours of gloom and peril.
   Guide, pathfinder of nations—we salute thee, hail, all hail to thy name.
4. When the night was thick with darkness and the country sick and prostrate with grief—thy benediction, even then, was constant in the land and looked with calm, unwavering eyes upon us. And thou saved'st us, mother, when we were encompassed with fears and fearsome perils.
   Healer of the woes of nations, king of our country's fate—we salute thee, hail, all hail to thy name.
5. Day dawns at last, and the level rays of the sun strike the brows of the eastern hill. Birds sing, and the breeze pours new life into our soul. In the sunshine of thy mercy. O Lord, our sleeping people wake—their heads lowly beneath thy feet.
   Lord of our kingdoms, king of our country's fate—we salute thee, hail, all hail to thy name.

Note: In the first line of the poem, the word "fate" was misprinted as "gate". All spellings are as published.

It is amply clear from the English translation that the song was in praise of the British King and no one else.

Immediately after the song, the Congress president himself moved the following resolution:

"This Congress in humble duty, respectfully tenders its most loyal homage to the throne and person of Their Imperial Majesties, the King Emperor and the Queen Empress and feels confident that their visit to India will be productive of lasting benefit to the people of this country."[40]

The resolution was carried, unanimously.

"As soon as the cheering subsided the organ again struck and a Hindi song, paying heart-felt homage to their Imperial Majesties was sung by Bengali boys and girls in a chorus."[40]

Only after these three items,

1. Song of Rabindranath, Jana Gana Mana;
2. Resolution tendering loyal homage to the King and the Queen;
3. Hindi song paying homage to their Imperial Majesties;

were over, other business of the day merited attention. These three items of welcome to the King and Queen were not interrupted by any other activity.

Surendranath Banerjee was born in the year 1848, and entered the elite services, the ICS, at the age of 23. There were some allegations and after three years of service, he was dismissed. Undaunted he established a college, 'Ripon College' after Lord Ripon, the Viceroy of India. He was aware of the power of a newspaper and started *The Bengalee*, which was published daily from Calcutta. He was also the editor of the paper. He was a close friend of Rabindranath and always allotted him prominent and ample space in his paper. He was a staunch supporter of the British Government and submitted to their wishes to such an extent that Bengalis nicknamed him Surrender Nath. Even at the age of 58, he thought nothing of fighting at Surat, with nationalists, by shoes, along with his other moderate friends. The British Raj had a system of rewarding the faithful. He became a member of the Imperial Legislative Council and in 1919, a minister of Local self-government.

When the song 'Jana Gana Mana' was presented, Surendranath was the only one who considered it a patriotic song. At that time there were many English and Vernacular papers, but none of them described the song as patriotic. Even the author never recognised it as a patriotic song; then why did Surendranath, a well-educated and informed man, described the song as patriotic?

The word patriotism is derived from the Greek word—Patris, meaning fatherland. Patriotism means love and loyal support to the fatherland. Up to this point there is universal agreement, but when patriotism is further defined, two different views emerge.

The first view explains that patriotism involves loyalty to the government of the day. All citizens should loyally support all government policies and actions. It is the patriotic duty of every citizen to remain loyal to the ruler of the nation. If the head of the government is a king, then the same unflinching loyalty is to be shown to him. The second view maintains that a true patriot will not support the government of the day, if it is unjust and unwise. If the government is headed by a tyrannical king then, even revolt against him is an act of patriotism. A famous British critic, Samuel Johnson, wrote, "Patriotism is the last refuge of a scoundrel". Surendranath took such a refuge, and found Jana Gana Mana, a patriotic song.

The Congress of 1911 was completely dominated by moderates such as Surendranath, who believed in the first view. The Congress president of the same year said from the dais "...if we appeal to it (British royal authority) ... and convince it by our persistent and patriotic endeavours... it will never fail to respond to our appeal."[41] Like all other moderates, the Congress president was also of the view that loyalty to the British king was patriotism. Nationalists like Balgangadhar Tilak and his friends, who could have challenged and opposed Jana Gana Mana, were all behind bars in British jails.

For Surendranath, praise for the King Emperor could be nothing else except patriotism, but it was the patriotism of a slave for his master. Jana Gana Mana was a song which praised the virtues of the slave master.

9

Flaw in the Song Jana Gana Mana

The Cause of its Rejection

The despotic rule of the East India Company came to an end after the 1857 War of independence, and the much alarmed British Parliament enacted the Government of India Act of 1858, by which the governing power was transferred from the John Company to the British Crown. India was divided into two parts; British India, governed directly by the British Crown and the Indian States, ruled and managed by the Indian princes.

The British Crown dealt with the Indian princes, with respect. Dalhousie's infamous 'Doctrine of Lapse' of was quietly abandoned, and the right of the Indian princes to adopt an heir, was once again restored. In the year 1858, Lord Canning, the existing Viceroy of India, was reappointed by the Crown as the Governor General and Viceroy of British India. On November 1, 1858, he held a Durbar at Allahabad to declare the assumption of the Government of India by the British Crown. On that occasion a proclamation of Queen Victoria was read by him, and this proclamation became the basis by which India was administered for the next fifty years, till 1917. The proclamation, announced to the native princes of India that "All treaties and engagements with them, by or under the authority of the Honourable East India Company are by us accepted and will be scrupulously maintained and we look for the like observance on their part. We desire no extension of our present territorial possession and while we will permit no aggression upon our dominions or our rights to be attempted with impunity, they shall sanction no encroachment on those of others. We shall respect the rights, dignity and honours of our Native Princes as our own, and we deserve that they, as well as our own subjects, should enjoy that prosperity and social advancement which can only be secured by internal peace and good governance."

The Allahabad Durbar was summoned in a hurry and it lacked the pomp and show that should have been evident in the durbar of the British Empire. The main objective of the Queen's proclamation and the Durbar was to assure the Indian princes that their territories would never be annexed in the future, and they would be treated with honour and dignity, by the British Crown. The proclamation served the desired purpose, but the British government was aware that Indians, especially the princes, were impressed most by magnificent shows and it looked forward to stage a show, the like of which was never seen before in India. The opportunity arose when the parliament led by Prime Minister Disraeli, the ever obliging friend of the Queen, passed the Act of 1876, by which Queen Victoria assumed the title of 'Empress of India'. At that time Lord Lytton was the Viceroy of India, and be decided to revive the Mughal traditions in a grand manner, for the formal declaration in India.

On the invitation of Queen Victoria, extended through the Viceroy, towards the end of 1876, Indian princes and their retinues assembled at Delhi, where Lord Lytton held an Imperial Durbar, and on the first day of January 1877, Queen Victoria assumed the title of "Empress of India".

Almost all the princes and rajas, totalling about 400, attended the impressive Imperial Durbar. At that time there were about 565 princes and rajas — who ruled states from as big as Hyderabad of 83,000 and Kashmir of 80,000 square miles to postage stamp-sized states, such as Kuba, Mengni and Jalia, all under five square miles.

Not to eliminate or assimilate any princely state became the most prominent Crown policy. No substantial efforts were ever made to interfere in the day-to-day running of a state, no matter how mismanaged it was. Some of them were very efficiently run, if not better than as well as any state of British India, while others were grossly mismanaged.

The survival of the British Raj was dependent on the cooperation of the princely states and the Delhi Durbar was one of the most effective exercises to ensure the perpetuation of that cooperation. While Dinkar Rao, Chief Minister of the Maharaja of Gwalior, was overwhelmed by the magnanimity and splendour of the great camp, it was the Maharaja of Indore, who summed up the feeling of his fellow princes. He informed the Viceroy: "India has been until now a vast heap of stones, some of them small. Now the house is built and from roof to the basement, each stone of it is in its right place"[42]

The activities of the Durbar lasted for several weeks and culminated in the afternoon of the first of January of 1877, with the proclamation of the Queen as the 'Empress of India'. Before the culmination of this extravagant event, the Viceroy personally and individually received the princes, on behalf of Her Majesty, the Queen of England. He made each prince sit, immediately below a full length portrait of the Queen, in complete regal regalia. The Viceroy then presented him a satin banner on the top of which was a British Imperial crown made of pure gold thread, and just below it was an expensively embroidered prince's Coat of

Arms. While presenting the banner, in a carefully worded speech, Lytton said: "I present Your Highness with this banner as a personal gift from Her Majesty, the Queen in commemoration of her assumption of the title of Empress of India. Her Majesty trusts that it may never be unfurled without reminding you not only of the close union between the throne of England and your loyal princely house, but also of the earnest desire of the paramount power to see your dynasty strong, prosperous and permanent". He then placed around the prince's neck, a big gold medal, engraved with the head of the Queen, attached by a crimson silk ribbon.

The assurance of the Viceroy was pregnant with tempting promises, especially in the last word 'Permanent'. This last word became the foundation stone of the much touted British policy, and whenever there was an occasion, or even without any occasion, the princely states were repeatedly reminded that "their existence is permanent, only as long as British Raj is there". Their policy of permanency paid rich dividends and almost all the 565 princely states at, least outwardly, remained loyal to the British Crown. As a result the political map of India of 1858 remained unchanged till August 14, 1947, the last day of the British Raj.

India of that time was actually two. One was British India and the other, princely states of India. For the ease of administration, British India was divided into seven convenient provinces, namely:

1. Punjab
2. Sind
3. Gujarat
4. Maratha - main city Bombay and formed Bombay Presidency.
5. Orissa - and adjoining areas.
6. Dravid - South India. Main city Madras and formed Madras Presidency.

Map

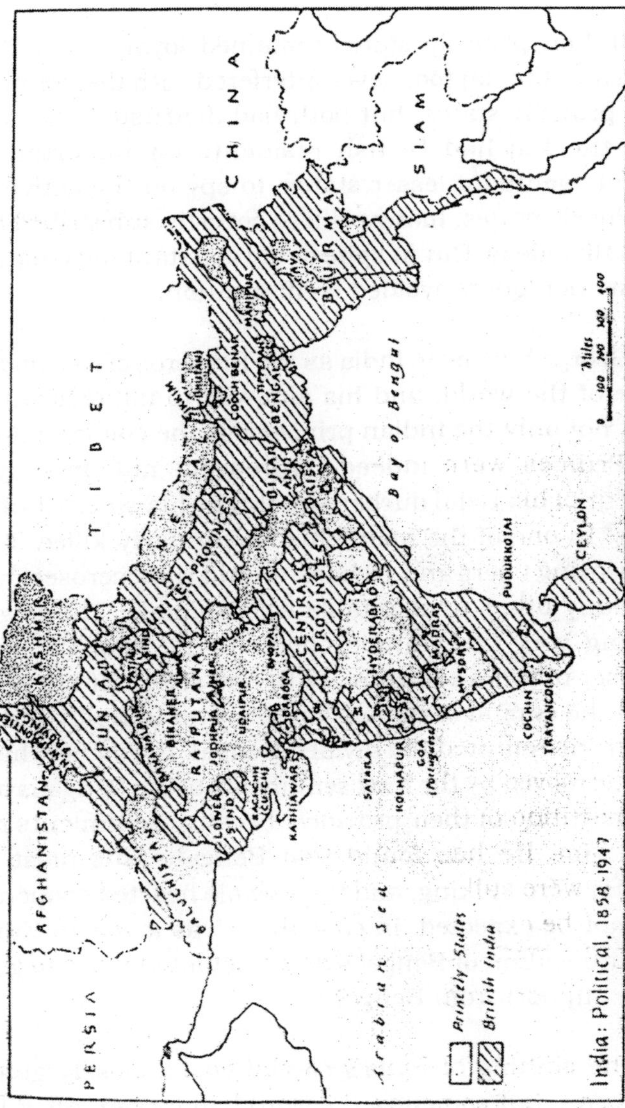

(Adapted from *Raj-The Making and Unmaking of British India* by Lawrence James. P. 329)

7. Bengal -Main city Calcutta, till 1911, capital of India and formed the largest Presidency.

Indian princely states remained loyal to the British Crown and the Raj too, never interfered with the boundaries of the princely states, but both had distrusted each other. While the Raj had British residents for important and political agents for lesser states, to spy on the activities of the princely states, many princes covertly subscribed to the nationalist ideas. But in spite of the constant mistrust, both sides meticulously avoided confrontation.

George V came to India as the Emperor of the mightiest empire of the world, and his aim was to impress with his might, not only the Indian princes but the common men as well. Princes were indeed impressed, not only by the grandeur of his Delhi durbar but also by his *shikar* (hunting) parties. In one of the many, his *shikar* party killed 39 fast disappearing tigers and 18 hard-to-find rhinoceroses[43] along with many other uncountable wild animals. The might of the King was truly unmatched, for he was the actual dispenser of India's destiny. With one stroke of his pen, he shifted the capital of India from Calcutta to Delhi and with another, he reunited the divided Bengal. It was not that the King was moved by the hurt sentiments of the Bengalis owing to the partition of their province, because sentiments never moved him. He had found that Bengalis, his most loyal subjects, were sulking, and their whole hearted cooperation could not be expected, in case there was a war in Europe. The reunification of Bengal was a calculated move to garner greater support from Bengal.

The shifting of India's capital was a closely guarded state secret, but somehow the word had leaked. All of Delhi was agog with the news that the King was going to restore the status and glory of the city, and after half a century, Delhi was again going to be the capital of India. From the days of Queen Victoria's durbar in 1877, such extravagant and lavish pageantry was never seen before in Delhi, or in any other city of India. Over one hundred thousand people witnessed the event, and about 20,000 participated in the activities of the durbar, and everyone, of any importance, was present there. The princes, led by the Maharaja of Bikaner, were there in droves, and even the head of the Pathuriaghat Tagores was there to hold a parasol over the royal head, then why was Babu Rabindranath from the Jorasanko family of Tagores, the family which had been loyal to the British Crown for five generations, not given the chance to present his loyal song Jana Gana Mana? Many explanations were given, and one of them was that the song was written in Bengali, a language which was not spoken or understood at Delhi. But that could not be a valid reason for the rejection of the song, as India was a multilingual country and Bengal was one of the favourite provinces of the Englishmen. Loyalty was encouraged by the British regime throughout the length and breadth of India and to recognise and reward the loyalty was a well established policy of the Raj. Then why was the devoted Rabindranath not accommodated in any one of the many functions of the durbar?

The Jana Gana Mana is a well balanced song and Rabindranath must have toiled for long hours to bring it to perfection. On close observation of the song, it is found that each verse has a set number of lines.

Verse V, has 6 lines.
Verse IV, has 6 lines.
Verse III, has 6 lines.
Verse II, has 6 lines.

In the same sequence, Verse I should also have six lines, but it is not so. It has seven lines, i.e. one additional line. The poet, obviously, must have patched the first verse with an extra line, and this one line must have been of utmost importance; otherwise the poet would not have spoiled the fine balance of his song. The line is "Punjab, Sind, Gujarat, Maratha, Dravid, Utkal, Banga," and it has seven words.

The song was composed in the classic 'Saar Chanda', also known as 'Narendra Lalit Pada', style [44] and the line:

पंजाब सिन्धु गुजरात मराठा द्राविड उत्कल बंगा

was not only extra, but had, when judged under the classic metre of 'Saar Chanda,' rendered the verse defective. The fault is caused by the presence of two more than the permitted 16 syllables in the line, because it starts with the word पंजाब which in the nomenclature of 'Chanda' is a 'Tagan' (तगण) [45] When this line is obliterated, the verse becomes a faultless 'Saar Chanda'. Rabindranath was very particular about the metre of his poetry, and he, almost never, allowed faults to creep into his verses. There must have been a great compulsion for him to tolerate this fault in the first verse of his poem 'Jana Gana Mana'. Probably, the original song was submitted to the National Committee without this one line of seven words. But without these seven words, the song was not acceptable to the committee.

The five verses of the song were masterly worded and painstakingly crafted to perfection in rhythm. The name of the royal couple was not to be seen, yet their majestic presence was felt throughout the song. George was depicted, not as a usual king but was elevated to the status of God, who was there to decide the fate of India. (Bharat =India, Bhagya=Fate, Bidhata=God). The song was crafted to titillate the egos of the king in a crescendo, and only towards the end, a perfect climax was reached, when 'India wakes up' and 'bends her head at thy feet' [verse V]. It was pure sycophancy in a sophisticated form, the like of which was, so far, never seen in Bengal. The poet was careful in not repeating the crudeness of his cousin, who had embarrassed many by his shameless sycophancy in his composition 'Victoria-Gitika'.[46]

In the original song, submitted to the National Committee, George was depicted as the God of India's destiny, which included not only British India but also the princely states. The song in its original form would have carried a misleading political message to the hundreds of princes, who had gathered at Delhi to participate in the coronation ceremonies, from all over India. Many of the princes, already primed with suspicion and mistrust, might have interpreted the signals from the song as George V's intention to bring the whole of India under British rule. The political advisors of the British Empire had probably rejected the song because of this serious flaw.

The promise given by the Viceroy Lytton, on behalf of the grandmother of George V, in the year 1876, was still fresh in the memory of many princes. They had travelled over long distances, after unfurling the satin banner with the imperial crown presented to them by Lytton, and many had come with a glittering gold medal dangling from their necks by a crimson silk ribbon. King George knew that the crowned head of his grandmother, engraved on the gold medal, was a silent witness to the assurances given by England, to the wearer of it. The British Empire had no intention of getting the importance of Her Majesty's promise undermined by a song of a, then, unknown and obscure Bengali poet.

After realising his omission, Rabindranath added in the first verse the names of all the seven provinces which formed the British India. That is why only the first verse has seven, and all the other verses have six lines. With this addition, the jurisdiction of the 'Dispenser of India's destiny' was limited to British India only, and the revised song was now acceptable to the Empire.

The early flags of India also recognised her as a nation of seven provinces, and long before Mohandas Karamchand

Gandhi said, "It will be necessary for us Indians, Hindus, Muslims, Christians, Jews, Parsis and all others to whom India is their home, to recognise a common flag to live and die for", many flags had been designed for India. In all these flags, British India was symbolically represented by seven figures; one figure for each province. The earliest known national flag of India is believed to have been unfurled in Paris by the revolutionary Madame B.R.Cama, in the year 1905. It consisted of three horizontal strips. The top most strip had seven stars, each star representing one province of the British India. The same flag was also exhibited in 1907 at an International Socialist Congress held at Stuttgart, Germany. The first flag on Indian soil was hoisted in the year 1906. However, by this time, the province of Bengal was divided into two, and it too reflected in the flag. Like the first, this flag was also tricolour but the upper strip had eight lotuses because at that time British India had eight provinces. This flag was hoisted on 7th August, in the Parse Bagan Square, which is now known as Green Park of Kolkata. In the year 1917, Dr. Annie Besant conceptualised another flag. The King of England in 1911 had unified the two provinces of Bengal and once again, British India had seven provinces, and so, this flag – unfurled by Dr. Annie Besant along with Lokmanya Tilak during the Home Rule movement – had seven stars, one star for each province.

It is abundantly clear that the India of Jana Gana Mana was not all of India, but only the British part of India, which consisted of seven provinces, namely:

1. Punjab, 2. Sind, 3. Gujarat, 4. Maratha, 5. Dravid (South India—Madras province), 6. Utkal (Orissa) and 7. Bengal.

The 'Bharat Bhagaya Bidhata' had under his command only the destiny of British India and not the rest of India *(See map on page 77)* which comprised over 565 princely states. Some princely states like Kashmir, Rajputana, Hyderabad and Mysore were as big as any province of British India. Other important states were Travancore, Patiala, Nabha, Jind, Kathiawar and Manipur. Not a single one of these important and prominent states found its name in the song Jana Gana Mana; for the simple reason that all these states were not part of British India. In the song, only the seven provinces of British India "pray for thy blessing", (verse I, Line 8) and not a single one of over 565 princely states of India joins them, in this prayer.

10

Analysis of the Song

Truth Must Prevail

It was decided to begin the second day of the Indian National Congress session, with homage to the King Emperor and Empress, and the song Jana Gana Mana was the first on the list. The song was sung well but was not properly understood, for it was in Bengali, the local vernacular language. Pandit Bishan Narayan was the Congress president, and although he was from the United Provinces, but as the close friend of Surendranath knew the genesis of the song. The Congress of that time was firmly and totally in the hands of the moderates. This session of Congress was attended by 446 delegates from all over India and all of them were moderates, as the nationalists were barred from even entering the venue from the days of Surat fiasco. The song was the first item of the day and not all the delegates were present to greet the song. Rabindranath left after the song was over, without submitting a customary copy of it. The official Congress report of 27th Dec'1911 states, "The proceedings commenced with a patriotic poem composed by Babu Rabindranath Tagore..." No details of the poem were given as the copy of the song was not submitted.

In circa 1911, several newspapers were published from Calcutta, some owned by Englishmen, others by Bengalis. They all, in detail, reported on the 26th session of Congress, which was an important event of the city. Staff reporters from most of the papers were present there to report on the activities of the Congress session. There was even one from the Reuters news team, which had arrived from England to cover the tour of the royal couple.

The Englishman of December 28, 1911 reporting on the events of December 27 wrote: "The proceedings began with a song of welcome to the King Emperor, specially composed by Babu Rabindranath Tagore".

"The Bengali poet Babu Rabindranath Tagore sang a song, composed by him specially to welcome the Emperor," said the *Statesman* of December 28.

The Indian in the issue of the December 29 wrote: "When the proceedings of the Indian National Congress began on Wednesday, December 27, 1911 a Bengali song in welcome of the Emperor was sung. A resolution welcoming the Emperor and Empress was also adopted unanimously".

International news agency 'Reuters' correspondent reported "The proceedings of the Indian National Congress began on December 27, 1911 by a song of welcome to the Emperor and the Empress. The song was composed and sung by a Bengali poet, Babu Rabindranath Tagore".

All these sources, independent and unrelated to each other, were of the same opinion, that the song Jana Gana Mana was composed by Babu Rabindranath to welcome the King George and his wife.

There were only two papers, both from Calcutta, which reported differently. One was *Amrit Bazaar Patrika*, which was originally published from Jessore. The owner of it was critical of the British government, so he was jailed for criticising the government and the printing press was locked. In 1871, it was shifted to Calcutta and *Patrika* was once again in circulation, but the harassment of the owner continued and the paper was once again gagged by the Empire. Left with no alternative, it was sold to a Crown loyalist, and the paper became pro-British, and this was the paper which declared that Jana Gana Mana was "... a song of benediction". The dictionary meaning of benediction is "utterance of blessings at the end of church service", which is like asking for favours from God. For *Patrika* the King was no less than God, and the song which "prays for thy blessing and sing thy praise" [verse one] could be nothing else but a song of benediction. The *Patrika* was not alone and this view was shared by many, who also regarded the British King, a living God. Muralidhar Roy, a prominent Congressman, declared from the Congress dais: "We Indians look upon the sovereign as part of Divinity and our loyalty and attachment to him is only natural".[40] The Congress General Secretary W.E. Wacha was also of the same opinion, and he said, "by the modification of partition (of Bengal) a great act of injustice had been repaired ... by a modern trinity—not a trinity of Indian Gods but of British Gods, His Gracious Majesty the King Emperor, the Secretary of State and the Viceroy"[40]

From these utterances, it is abundantly clear that for those who were loyal to the British Crown, the King was no less than God. Naturally for them, the song asking for his blessings was a song of benediction.

The second paper was *The Bengalee* which was published and edited by none else than Surendranath Banerjee, a staunch Crown loyalist and a moderate Congressman. He regarded himself, like other moderates, a British subject, and for him the praise of the King could be nothing else but a display of patriotism. On December 28, 1911, his paper reported, "The proceedings opened with a patriotic song composed by Babu Rabindranath Tagore..."[40]. But this was not the patriotism of an Indian for his nation; it was the patriotism of a slave for his slave master.

Surendranath was the only one, who had a copy of the song, given to him by his friend Babu Rabindranath. He was prepared, and the next day, in a sort of scoop, *The Bengalee* was the only paper, which was able to print the English translation of the song.

The Song and its Meanings

The song, written in 'Saar Chanda' style, consists of five verses, and each one has six lines, except the first, which has seven lines.

The song appears in many different formats, but this configuration is as it appears in *Gitabitan*, a book of songs by Rabindranath.[172]

The original song in Devanagri script.

जन गण मन

जनगणमन – अधिनायक जय हे भारत–भाग्यविधाता।
पंजाब सिन्धु गुजरात मराठा द्राविड़ उत्कल बंगा
विंध्य हिमाचल यमुना गंगा उच्छल – जलधितरंगा
तव शुभ नामे जागे, तव शुभ आशिष मांगे
गाहे तव जयगाथा।
जनगण–मंगलदायक जय हे भारत– भाग्यविधाता।
जय हे, जय हे, जय हे, जय जय जय, जय हे।।

(2)

अहरह तव आह्वान प्रचारित, शुनि तब उदार वाणी
हिंदु बौद्ध सिख जैन पारसिक मुसलमान ख्रिस्टानी
पूरब पश्चिम आसे तब सिंहासन–पाशे
प्रेमहार हय गाथा।
जनगण–ऐक्य–विधायक जय हे भारत–भाग्यविधाता।

जय हे, जय हे, जय हे, जय जय जय, जय हे।।

(3)

पतन–अभ्युदय बंधुर पन्था युगयुगधावित यात्री,
हे चिरसारथि, तव रथचक्रे–मुखरित पथ दिन रात्रि
दारूण–विप्लव माझै, तव शंखध्वनि बाजे
संकटदुःखत्राता।
जनगण–पथपरिचायक जय हे भारत–भाग्यविधाता।
जय हे, जय हे, जय हे, जय जय जय, जय हे।।

(4)

घोर तिमिरघन निबिड़ निशीथे पीड़ित मूर्छित देशे
जाग्रत छिल तव अविचल मंगल नतनयने अनिमेषे।
दुःस्वप्ने आंतके रक्षा करिले अंके,
स्नेहमयी तुमि माता।
जनगण–दुःखत्रायक जय हे भारत–भाग्यविधाता।
जय हे, जय हे, जय हे, जय जय जय, जय हे।।

(5)

रात्रि प्रभातिल, उदिल रविच्छवि पूर्व उदयगिरिभाले,
गाहे विहंगम, पुण्य समीरण नवजीवन रस ढाले।
तव करूणारूण–रागे निद्रित भारत जागे
तव चरणे नत माथा।
जय जय जय हे, जय राजेश्वर, भारत–भाग्य विधाता।
जय हे, जय हे, जय हे, जय जय जय, जय हे।।

In 1919, Tagore went on a tour of South India, where he stayed as the guest of James H. Cousins, the Principal of the Theosophical College at Madanapalle. There at the request of the Principal, he sang Jana Gana Mana for the students of the college, but many in the audience could not understand the meaning of the song as it was in Bengali. The Principal requested the poet to translate the song into English, so that English-speaking people could also understand the song. The poet accepted the request and the English rendering of the song was produced by Rabindranath himself.

In the English rendering, the poet made a few changes and attempted to dilute the sycophancy of the original

Bengali song. The original song had a total number of 206 words and, out of these, one-fifth was the word *Jaya*, which is an often used word for praise and it was repeated for 44 times in the song. But in the English rendering, even though the total numbers of words were 304, the use of the word 'Victory' (equivalent of *Jaya*) was reduced to only 15. In the original song, the King was presented as *Bidhata* (God) of India's destiny, while in the English rendering he is reduced to an ordinary 'Dispenser' of India's destiny.

English Rendering By Rabindranath Tagore:

[I]

Thou art the ruler of the minds of all people,
Thou Dispenser of India's destiny,
Thy name rouses the hearts of Punjab, Sind, Gujrat
and Maratha, of Dravida, Orissa and Bengal.
It echoes in the hills of the Vindhyas and Himalayas.
mingles in the music of Jamuna and Ganges, and is
chanted by the waves of the Indian Sea.
They pray for thy blessing and sing thy praise,
Thou Dispenser of India's destiny,
Victory, Victory, Victory to thee.

[II]

Day and night, thy voice goes out from land to land,
calling Hindus, Buddhists, Sikhs and Jains round
thy throne and Parsees, Mussalmans and Christians,
Offerings are brought to thy shrine by the East and the
West to be woven in a garland of love.
Thou bringest the hearts of all peoples into harmony
Of one life,
Thou Dispenser of India's destiny,
Victory, Victory, Victory to thee.

[III]

Eternal Charioteer, thou drivest man's history along
The road rugged with rises and falls of Nations.
Amidst all tribulations and terror thy trumpet sounds
to

hearten those that despair and droop and guide all
people in their paths of peril and pilgrimage.
Thou Dispenser of India's destiny,
Victory, Victory, Victory to thee.

[IV]

When the long dreary night was dense with gloom
and the country lay still in a stupor,
thy Mother's arms held her,
thy wakeful eyes bent upon her face,
till she was rescued
from the dark evil dreams
that oppressed her spirit,
thou Dispenser of India's destiny,
Victory, Victory, Victory to thee.

[V]

The night dawns, the sun rises in the East,
the birds sing, the morning breeze
brings a stir of new life.
Touched by the golden rays of thy love
India wakes up and
bends her head at thy feet.
Thou King of all kings,
Thou Dispenser of India's destiny,
Victory, Victory, Victory to thee.

The Song in Roman script

1. Jano gano mano adhinayaka jayahe Bharata bhagya Bidhata, Punjabo Sindhu Gujrato Maratha Drabino Utkala Bango Bindhyo Himachalo Jamuna Ganga Uchhalo jalodihi tarango Tabo subho namay jagay, Tabo subho ashiso mangay, Gahay tabo jayagatha, Jano gano mangala daayaka Jayahey Bharata Bhagya Bidhat Jayahey, jayahey, jayahey, Jaya jaya jaya jayahey.
2. Aharaha tabo awhbano pracharito, Shuni tabo udaro bani Hindu Bauddho Sikho Jaino Parasiko Musalmano

Khristani Puraba Pashchimo aashay Tabo singhasano pashay Premoharo hawye gantha Jano gano oikya bidhyaka jayahey Bharata Bhagya Bidhata Jayahey, jayahey, jayahey, Jaya jaya jaya jayahey.

3. Patana-abhyudaya bandhuro pantha Jugo jugo dhabito jatri, Hey chiro sarathi, tabo ratha chakreMukharito patha dino ratri Daruna biplaba majhay Tabo shankha dhwani bajay Sankata Dukho trata Jano gano patha parichyaka Jayahey Bharata Bhagya Bidhata Jayahey, jayahey, jayahey, Jaya jaya jaya jayahey.

4. Ghoro timiro ghono nibiro nishithay Pirito murchhito deshay Jagrata chhilo tabo abichalo mangaloNato nayanay animeshay Duhswapnay atankay Rakkha karilay ankay Snehamayee tumi mata Jano gano- dukho trayaka jayahey Bharata Bhagya Bidhata Jayahey, jayahey, jayahey, Jaya jaya jaya jayahey

5. Ratri prabhatilo, udilo rabichhabi Purbo udaya giri bhalay Gahav bihangamo punyo samirano, Nabo jibana rasa dhalay Tabo karunaruno ragay Nidrito Bharata jagay Tabo Charne nath matha Jaya jaya jayahey, Jaya rajeswara Bharata Bhagya Bidhata, Jayahey, jayahey, jayahey, jaya jaya jaya jayahey.

An English translation of the original song was published in *The Bengalee* paper on 28th Dec' 1911 (see page 67). There were many changes in the translated version, published by *The Bengalee*, and when this version of the song is read, it becomes clear that it was written to welcome and praise the British King. In the translation, 'Bidhata, that is God' was shown as an ordinary 'King' and it was the 'King of our country's fate, we salute' (verse one of translated song). In verse five, the words are, 'In the sunshine of thy mercy, O Lord, our sleeping people wake — their heads lowly beneath thy feet'. These 'sleeping people' are no one else but the unfortunate Indians. The word 'Bharat' (India), though repeated seven times in the original song, is not to be seen in the translation. It was replaced by 'Country' to avoid any controversy with the princely states of India.

Meaning of the song—when the meaning of the song is sought it is some what like this:

[1]

Hail you, who control the fate of India and rule over her people and their hearts. Punjab, Sind, Gujarat, Maharashtra, South India, Orissa and Bengal provinces, along with Himalaya and Vindhyachal mountains , and the rivers Ganga Jamuna and the Indian sea, they all together, wake up and sing your praises and ask for your blessings. You are the harbinger of good fate to India, victory to you.

[2]

Whenever you call Hindus, Buddhists, Sikhs, Jains, Muslims and Christians, gather by your side and stand united. Hail you, who have brought unity to the people of India.

[3]

You have written the history of our nation, which is full of many ups and downs. You are our eternal guide and through ages we have followed you with the devotion of a pilgrim, victory to you, who has saved us from fear and misery.

[4]

When this country was sick and paralysed with gloom and fear, you, our kind mother, saved us from the fearful nightmares and protected us from miseries.

[5]

Night is over and it is day again. Birds are now singing and one can feel the invigorating morning breeze. Stirred by your compassionate voice, sleeping India wakes up and bends her head under your feet. You, who are king of all kings, may always be victorious.

In all the five verses of the song, nowhere is any praise for India to be found. Moreover, there is not a single word of glorification for the motherland. Nowhere, does the song instil a feeling of pride, and fills the hearts of people with patriotism and loyalty, which are the basic requirements of a national anthem. On the contrary, from the beginning to the end, this song depicts India as a worthless nation which is filled with gloom, dreaming of dark evils and is in a state of stupor [verse IV]. In the next verse, this worthless nation is 'touched by the golden rays of thy love' and then, she is made to do a most shameful act. India, our motherland, the country of our pride, the nation for the honour of which millions of us have willingly sacrificed their lives, our beloved

'India wakes up and
Bends her head at thy feet.
Thou Kings of all Kings,
Thou Dispenser of India's destiny' [Verse V]

Today, the millions of proud Indians will willingly sacrifice their lives, but will not allow any to bend the head of Mother India, at the feet of a King.

After the song was recited, many started to realise that 'Bharat Bhagya Bidhata' was none but the British King, and this worried Rabindranath and his friends. They were aware that nationalist Indians may mark him, as one of the many sycophants that the Tagore clan had produced. As a Pirali, he was already shunned by the high-caste Hindus, and he feared that with the stigma of a sycophant, even the commoner might start avoiding him.

To confuse the people and stop them from realising the truth, many stories were invented and several explanations were circulated, but when the song is carefully examined, three truth indicators are found, and these indicators were inbuilt in the song by the poet himself. All the stories, statements and explanations, when seen in the light of these three truth indicators, turn out to be poorly concocted lies.

The first truth Indicator—This indicator is embedded in the first verse, in which the poet says: "Thy name rouses the hearts of the Punjab, Sind, Gujarat and Maratha, of Dravid, Orissa and Bengal." Whoever was the character of the song, his name could "rouse the hearts" of only the British part of India, which consisted of these, above mentioned, seven provinces. The character of the song had no power over the rest of India, which comprised over 565 princely states like Kashmir and Hyderabad. Without these 565 states, India was only half complete. The character of the song had his writ run, with God like powers, only in this half of India.

The first truth indicator is that the character of the song could be only the one, who had his absolute power over the British part of India.

The second truth indicator—Rabindranath at the mature age of seventy years, in 1930, told an audience at Oxford University: "The unconventional code of life for our family has been a confluence of three cultures, Hindu, Mohammedan and British"[47]

Indeed, Rabindranath's forefathers were very close to Muslims, specially the one with the name of Pir Ali, a powerful minister of the Nawab of Bengal, and for their closeness with him, they came to be known as Pirali Thakur. After the Muslims, the Tagores became intimate with the

British, and were in their close contact for several generations. For the ease of pronunciation by British tongues, they even changed their family name from Thakur to Tagore. Rabindranath's father, Maharishi Devendranath renounced Hindu Dharma and formally joined Brahmo Samaj, which was nothing but a form of Christianity, modified for the Hindus. Thus, Tagore knew well, the intricacies of the Muslim and Christian religions, and that it was sacrilegious for Muslims, as well as for Christians, to make offerings at a shrine, yet he wrote:

"...Mussalmans and Christians.
Offerings are brought to thy shrine..." [Verse two]

The first and second commands of sacrosanct Decalogue, commonly known as Ten Commandments, are:

1. I am the Lord thy God, thou shalt have no other God before me.

2. Thou shalt not make unto thee any graven image, or any graven likeness of any that is in heaven above, or that in the earth beneath, or that is in the water under the earth.

Thus, every Christian is commanded by God himself to have no other God, and is forbidden to bring offerings to a shrine of any other form of God.

The Holy Quran directs all the Muslims to:

"Worship Allah and join none with Him (in worship)"[48]

The Holy Quran also warns the faithful:

"Whoever sets up partners with Allah in worship, he has indeed invented a tremendous sin"[49]

When doubts were raised about the identity of the 'Bharat Bhagaya Bidhata', many were told that he was a 'deity', and Rabindranath himself explained him as an 'eternal charioteer', but it was not possible for Christians and Muslims to bring their offerings to the shrine of a deity or of a charioteer. On the other hand, both were not only permitted, but it was traditional to make offerings to their King.

The second truth indicator is that the character of the song can only be someone, for whom Muslims and Christians are permitted to bring their offerings.

The third truth Indicator—the song consists of five verses and the last portion of each verse,

'Bharat Bhagaya Bidhata
Jayahe Jayahe Jayahe, Jaya Jaya Jaya Jayahe'

is the same. These are the rhythm lines, repeated at the end of each verse, regardless of its contents, and it is a much used feature of many songs. Apart from these rhythm lines, the remaining portion of each verse is addressed to a masculine figure, except in verse IV. This entire verse IV is unmistakably addressed to a feminine figure. For example, its two lines:

Dukswapney atankay rakksha karilay ankay
Snehmayee tumi *mata.*

(English meaning: Through the fearful nightmares, you protected us on your lap. You, the *mother,* who is full of love)

No matter, how these two lines are interpreted, the word *Mata* can only mean a female figure, *Mother.*

In all the other verses—with the sole exception of verse IV—the song is addressed to a man and only masculine words are used. For example, the word "Rajeshwara" of verse V, means King of Kings, and is undoubtedly a masculine word.

The third truth indicator is that the song depicts two different characters, one male and one female.

11

Lies Associated with the Song

The Aim was to Confuse and Camouflage the Truth

As soon as the song was out, many lies started circulating, to mask the truth. The lies were:

1. **It was a patriotic song**: Only one man, Surendranath, labelled the song as patriotic. As discussed earlier, *The Bengalee*, which was owned and edited by him, was the only paper which declared it patriotic. There was not an iota of patriotism in it, for the nation, and whatever praise and glorification was there, was for the British royal couple.

In fact it was a song in which slave mother, "...India wakes up and bends her head at thy feet. Thou King of all Kings" [verse V]

The Congress recorded Jana Gana Mana as a patriotic song, but this patriotism was that of a slave, for his master. In the song there is no patriotism or glorification of India. On the contrary, she has been repeatedly ridiculed and insulted.

2. **It was a song of benediction**: So declared *Amrit Bazar Patrika*, a paper published from Calcutta. The existence

of the paper, as already discussed, was dependent on the mercy of the white men, so their king was no less than a God for the paper. For it, a song which "... prays for thy blessing and sing thy praise" [Verse I, Eng. rendering], could only be a song of benediction.

3. **The song was addressed to a deity**: This was a widely circulated story, which even today is accepted by many as truth. The story is about W.B. Yeats, the poet who had helped Rabindranath with *Gitanjali,* and wrote an introduction for it. According to the story, Yeats was disturbed when he came to know that Rabindranath had written a song in the honour of King George. One of Tagore's Bengali friends, who was on a visit to London told Yeats as to how the song was created.

"The national committee came to Mr. Tagore and asked him to write some thing for the Delhi Durbar. And as you know Mr. Tagore is very obliging. And all that afternoon be tried to write them a poem and he could not. And that evening the poet as usual retired to his meditation. And in the morning he descended with a sheet of paper. He said "Here in the poem I have written. It is addressed to the deity. But you may give it to the national committee. Perhaps it will content them"[50]

Friends of Tagore knew that the poem was addressed to a deity and not to the King of Britain.

W.B. Yeats told this story to Ezra Pound, who was the foreign correspondent of the magazine *Poetry* published from Chicago. Pound then recounted this story to his father in America, through a letter.

This was a story based on hearsay and never endorsed by Rabindranath, but such was his spell that a large section of Indians believed in it. In this story the name of Tagore's Bengali friend was not mentioned, in a true story names are given. The story was told to Yeats, who told it to Ezra Pound, who then told it to his father, who in the end told it to others before the story was out. The story was only gossip which travelled in circles and crossed continents in the hope of acquiring some element of truth, but failed.

The song could never have been written for a deity, for it is a religious word of the Hindus, and is always gender specific. The masculine deity is known as Devta (He deity) and the feminine deity is called Devi (She deity). In a song, the same deity can never be addressed by masculine words in some stanzas and by feminine expressions in others. Moreover it is blasphemy for Christians and Muslims to make offerings at a shrine of a Hindu deity.

4. **The song was addressed to the Eternal Charioteer**: The song Jana Gana Mana was first presented in the year 1911, and immediately afterwards doubts about the identity of the 'Bharat Bhagaya Bidhata' began surfacing. By almost all the papers of Calcutta, the mega-city where Tagore lived, the poem was reported as a song of welcome to King George V. Rabindranath must have read these reports published in the various papers of Calcutta, but he never contradicted any of them, and always avoided all the questions that required him to disclose the identity of the 'Bharat Bhagaya Bidhata'. Rabindranath kept evading all such questions, not for one or two years, or for one or two decades, but for as many as 26 years.

In 1937, when a correspondent drew his attention to the claim that Jana Gana Mana was actually composed to honour the King of England, Rabindranath replied: "In this song, I have proclaimed the victory of that Eternal Charioteer who drives man's destiny along the road rugged with the rises and falls of nations. That Great Dispenser of human destiny through the ages could never be George the fifth or George the sixth, or for that matter any other George".

When in 1939, Rabindranath was again confronted with a similar question, and his answer was almost the same. The only difference was that this time the correspondent was rebuked. Tagore observed: "I should only insult myself if I cared to answer those who consider me capable of such unfounded stupidity as to worship George the fourth or George the fifth as the Eternal Charioteer..."

In those years, India was under British rule and Rabindranath was not an ordinary person. He was a knight of the British Empire and Prima Donna of the Raj, which was still strong and kicking. To cross examine such a VVIP required such courage which the native reporters of that time were not allowed to have. No one dared to ask any more questions, regarding the origin of the song.

It must be admitted that in 1939, though he was 79 years old; Tagore was still capable of bringing out sufficient sentimental arguments to bury the truth, but can truth ever be buried?

सत्यमेव जयते नानरितम—मुनदाक उपनिशद

(Truth alone prevails, not untruth—Mundaka Upanishad)

Rabindranath, as the writer of the song, should have answered the question of the correspondent in greater detail. In his reply the poet referred to "... Eternal Charioteer who drives man's destiny along the road rugged with the rises and falls of nations ..." When answering, the poet was talking not of one nation but of nations, which gave the impression that in the song he meant a charioteer of the whole world. In fact, even if we presume that the character of the song was a charioteer, he still could not have been for the whole world, because he represented not even one complete nation, but only seven provinces, which completed only half of India — the British part of India. Even if the shrine mentioned in the song was accepted as that of an Eternal Charioteer, the poet still had to explain the blasphemy of Christians and Muslims, when they were made to bring their offering to his shrine. If the song was about an Eternal Charioteer, how could that charioteer be a female, Mata, in one stanza and a male, Rajrajeshwar, in the next?

For as many as 26 years, Rabindranath did not respond to any query that required him to comment upon the identity of the 'Bharat Bhagaya Bidhata'. Some unusual event must have occurred, towards the end of this period, which changed the situation, so that in 1937, it was no longer necessary for Rabindranath to avoid the question. In fact, during all these years the actual Bharat Bhagaya Bidhata was alive. King George V died in the year 1936, and only then Rabindranath dared to make the claim that the song was about an Eternal Charioteer. With the death of the King the hesitation was gone, because the dead George could not arise from his grave to contradict the poet. Had George V lived a few more years and died after Rabindranath, the history of our national anthem would have been different.

12

The Rise of Rabindranath Tagore

Fear of World War Did It

When the King of England, in 1911, visited India, the clouds of war could be seen over the European sky, and they were getting darker with every passing day. They were in the making for the last several years, and if the thick pile of the intelligence reports, on the imperial desk, was to be believed, war was imminent. Many European nations, especially Germany, were bitterly envious of British prosperity and the glory of her Empire. Though there was no immediate danger to the island nation, her colonial territories, the fountainhead of her wealth, were definitely at risk.

King George V was never known for the brightness of his ideas or the acumen of his political decisions, but the well-being of the British Empire was always at the top in his thinking. He was aware that in the likely event of the war breaking out in Europe, the British government would be required, not only to shift from India as many British soldiers as it was possible, but also to recruit a great number of Indians in the royal army, to fight and die for the British cause. To make the idea acceptable to the Indians, it was imperative for the Empire to win over, as many political leaders and intellectuals in India, as was possible. The nationalists, whose patriotism was for their motherland India, led by Bal Gangadhar Tilak and Sardar Ajit Singh, were behind bars. As a result, for many years no nationalist activity was seen in the country. The Indian political scenario was dominated by moderates, who were loyal to the British Crown. The moderates had a demand pending for the last several years which was fulfilled by the annulment of the partition of Bengal. It was accepted as a royal boon and had satisfied the moderates. Though the King was now not worried about the political leaders, yet there was not a single intellectual with the Empire, who was influential enough to mould the public opinion in favour of the Raj. The Indian intelligentsia of that time were either non-committal or nursed an anti-British feeling which was long ago implanted by Bankim Chandra Chatterjee. The immense popularity of Vande Mataram was the proof of it.

King George V arrived at Calcutta on December 30, 1911[52] and left on January 9, 1912. [53] During his ten days of stay at the then capital of India, he graced many receptions of honour, and presided over several meetings, called to discuss the affairs of the Raj. He already had, during his tour of India, many meetings with the Rajas, princes, British officials, Indian government functionaries, common and not so common men of his domain. From this interaction he found that the Indians were generally satisfied with the Raj, and perhaps would remain loyal to it. Still there was something which made him uneasy, and probably the stories of the 1857 revolt were the cause of it. He wanted the Indians to be even more loyal to the British Crown, so that they could never again think of revolting, and support the British openly, in case there was a war. In the past many tricks were tried which included the grant of honorary titles, Jagirs (land property) and lucrative government posts. The most preferred method to win over an intellectual was to patronise him, and then expect him to influence his fellow compatriots, in favour of the Raj. Rammohun Roy was one such example, but such tricks generally failed because the public could easily see the nexus between the man and the Empire. To be successful, it was essential to try a new approach with fresh ideas.

In Calcutta, the King had several private meetings with the Viceroy. Nothing unusual, as it was customary for the King to have such meetings. What transpired in these meetings can never be known because they were held without aides and written notes were never made, but it is known that the British King had undertaken the long and arduous journey of several thousand miles to garner greater support from India and ensure the loyalty of her people.

Soon, in the attitude of the Empire a sea change was seen, which overtook Rabindranath, unprepared and unsuspecting. He suddenly became persona grata for the same empire which only the previous month had found him unworthy of even reciting a poem, at the coronation Durbar of her King. The first gift of the Empire, to her new found primadonna, was an extravagantly arranged 50th birthday bash at the town hall of Calcutta. Only a few days earlier, the royal couple had left Calcutta, leaving everyone exhausted. Still the Empire insisted and the overtired worked overtime to arrange for, yet one more mega function.

The interest of the organisers of the function, in Rabindranath, was recent, otherwise they would not have missed his '50th year completion', which was eight months and twenty-two days earlier, because May 7, 1911 was the day when Rabindranath had actually completed his fiftieth year of life. The organisers were a group, known as 'Bangiya Sahitya Parishad', and they managed a library which functioned in a donated building. Their declared aim was to promote awareness for literature through the library, and at times they also honoured writers. Because of the meagre budget at their disposal, the functions were organised in a simple way, but when time came to honour Rabindranath, the Parishad became cash rich to hire the town hall, gift gold, silver, ivory and brocade, invite Maharajas, Princes, European judges and glitterati of the town. Present at the function were 'Maharaja of Sushan, Maharaja of Natore, Kumar Bahardur of Lalgoa, Mr. Justice Woodroffe and Mrs. Woodroffe, Sir Goorudas Banerjee, Sri Protul Chandra Chatterjee...' [54] and several hundreds more.

The date of the event was prominently advertised in the newspapers of Calcutta, and *The Bengalee* of January 25 carried this advertisement.

> "Bangiya Sahitya Parishad will meet at the Town Hall on day 28th Jan, 1912, at 4 PM for the ceremony of presenting an address to Babu Rabindranath Tagore on the occasion of his 50th year completion. Babu Sarada Charan Mitra M.A.B.L. will preside."

At the ceremony the President of the organisation, "presented a gold lotus" and the Secretary "a congratulatory address printed on ivory leaves, bound in the form of an antique Indian manuscript enclosed in a nice brocaded cloth". The Maharaja of Natore "...presented Argha in a Silver Sirvile".[54] In between there were many more gifts and addresses, felicitating the poet. The King left Calcutta on January 9 and the preparations for the function must have started from the very next day, for exactly after 19 days, the poet was honoured at this unique and impressive event which was unprecedented in the history of Calcutta.

On May 27, 1912, Rabindranath sailed to England, unaware that a very precious gift was waiting for him, in the heartland of the Empire. On this journey, Tagore was accompanied by his son and his son's wife Pratima. Tagore and party reached London on June16. There they had no friend or relative to stay with, so they all stayed in a Hotel at Bloomsbury, London. Rabindranath was soon to meet a person who was going to play an important role in his life, and change it, forever. This person settled Tagore in a rented house at Hampstead, and later on shifted him to an even more comfortable double storied villa at the posh Vale of Health residential area near central London. He not only looked after the material needs of Tagore, but tried hard to sell him in the literary circles of Britain. Overwhelmed with gratitude, Rabindranath dedicated the Nobel Prize winning *Gitanjali* to him. The name of that person was William Rothenstein. He was an artist by profession and had little interest in poets or their poetry. He once visited India to get acquainted with Indian paintings, and during this period had casually met Rabindranath. The meetings were cursory, and Tagore later was to tell his biographer Edward Thompson that Rothenstein "...did not know him as a poet at all, only as a member of the Tagore family".[55]

William, the painter had never before helped anyone the way he helped Tagore, who was a poet and not a painter. According to Rabindranath, Rothenstein "... had not been expecting him in London".[55] As a matter of fact, Rabindranath had never informed him about his intended visit to London, still " Rothenstein was fully expecting Tagore, had already planned a dinner for him and was involved in efforts to obtain an Oxford doctorate for him".[55] It was all strange. How Rothenstein came to know about Rabindranath's visit of and the way to locate him in a mega city like London? Moreover, Rothenstein never explained his interest in getting a doctorate—though he was not successful—for an unknown poet belonging to a distant land and an alien race. Rabindranath—or any one else in his family—had never requested Rothenstein to help in getting the doctorate from Oxford University. The actions of William became even stranger, when he on his own prevailed upon

Yeats to edit and improve *Gitanjali.* Yeats had initially refused to work upon *Gitanjali,* but it was not too difficult for William to persuade him. Again, it was Rothenstein who influenced India Society and Macmillan to publish *Gitanjali.* He also introduced Tagore to Sturge Moore, who was to recommend *Gitanjali* to the Swedish Academy, for the Nobel Prize. But the fondness of Rothenstein for Tagore was also sudden, and he too became flush with funds. London was always a very expensive city, as it is even today.[56] A fortune must have been spent to promote Rabindranath, and to look after the material needs of his several months long stay at London.

Like most of the painters of Europe, Rothenstein was not rich; still he was able to afford innumerable lavish parties hosted to establish Tagore in the literary circles of London. The most notable party was arranged at Trocadero restaurant, where along with Yeats, seventy more writers, critics and friends were wined and dined to appreciate the poems of Tagore.[55] This restaurant, situated near Piccadilly Circus of Central London, started business in the year 1896, and soon became one of the most exclusive places, not only in Britain but in the whole of Europe. It was so expensive that London could not afford it without the income from her Empire. It closed down with her disintegration in 1965.

Was there a hidden power orchestrating the show? No one can ever be sure, but it is known that Rothenstein's affection for Rabindranath was not to be seen again. When Tagore revisited London in 1920, he expected the same old warm welcome, but he was openly disappointed by the coldness of his old friend. Rothenstein loved paintings, and these were the passion of his life, but when Rabindranath invited him to visit 'Galerie Pigalle' in Paris, where his solo arts exhibition was to the inaugurated on May 2, 1930, Rothenstein declined. By William's actions, one is easily inclined to believe that he was given an assignment, and after its completion, Tagore did not deserve further attention.

Soon after the successful launching of Rabindranath as a poet, Rothenstein was given the lucrative Royal Commission to paint the scenes of the world war. He was later knighted, and when there was an opening in1920, he was awarded the coveted post of the Rector of the Royal College of Arts, where he remained till his retirement in 1935.

13

Rabindranath Repudiates Knighthood

He Never Did

It is often argued that William Rothenstein became cool towards Rabindranath, because he had repudiated the knighthood, and William regarded it as an insult to his country and the King. In the history of Britain, the knighthood has never been repudiated. The facts were different:

On 14th Nov'1913, Rabindranath received by telegram, the news of winning the Nobel Prize. Four days later, he wrote a letter to Rothenstein which became quite famous:

> "The perfect whirlwind of public excitement it has given rise to is frightful. It is almost as bad as tying a tin can to a dog's tail, making it impossible for him to move without creating noise"[57]

If the Nobel Prize was a tin can tied to the tail of a dog, the knighthood was a loyalty collar, clamped around its neck.

Rabindranath was well aware that the people of India looked with hate, upon the imperial titles and their holders.

Writes the official Congress magazine "For outstanding national treachery one could aspire to a Knighthood or even to a Jagir..."[58]

Knighthood was conferred upon Tagore in the year 1915, and from that very moment he was uneasy with it. He preferred to be called Gurudev and not Sir Rabindranath, but at that time Britain was in the midst of the First World War, and any attempt to refuse the knighthood would have been regarded as an act of subversion, by the British government, so he decided to wait. His chance came in the year 1919, when the world war was over, and the massacre of Jallianwala Bagh gave him an opportunity to regain his falling reputation.

The killings at Jallianwala Bagh occurred on 13th April, 1919, soon after Rabindranath drafted a letter to the Viceroy, Lord Chelmsford. In this letter of May 31, he wrote: "... The time has come when badges of honour make our shame glaring in the incongruous context of humiliation, and I, for my part wish to stand, shorn of all special distinctions."[59]

The Viceroy was not impressed, and wrote to the Secretary of State, Montagu "...I am unable myself, to relieve him of his title and in the circumstances, do not propose to make any recommendation to His Majesty on the subject." Edwin Montagu, after consulting the King, cabled back to ignore Tagore's request. Actually the decision to return the honour was taken in the heat of emotions, and when Tagore was explained of the great embarrassment that the British government would face after the surrender of the Knighthood, Rabindranath decided not to further pursue the matter. Had he insisted, there was no reason for not being successful in returning the title. Probably a tactical understanding was reached, that Tagore, never in future would raise the issue of surrendering the honour, and the government on its part would stop referring to him as Sir Rabindranath. He remained Sir Rabindranath, and even today his name is there in the official list.

The Indian political leadership of that time was aware of the drama played and the episode was not taken seriously. As a result, not a single national figure of importance, including Gandhi, Nehru or even C.R. Das, congratulated Tagore on his writing the letter to the Viceroy.

Rabindranath knew it. In 1921 be told his biographer Edwin Thompson. "I still have it. I have eaten my pudding and must keep it."[60]

Gandhi knew it. Provoked by some particularly acid comments by Tagore, he replied, referring to him as 'Sir Rabindranath',[61] as if reminding him of the loyalty collar which was still around his neck.

The English knew it. Goldsworthy Lowes Dickinson, a Cambridge friend of Tagore, wrote in a teasing letter to him 'Dear Sir Rabindranath Tagore, I call you so because I understand you have not yet succeeded in getting relieved of your unwelcome title".[62] When the poet died in 1941, all the papers of England in their obituaries referred to him as 'Sir Rabindranath'.

The Americans knew it. Whenever there was a reference to Tagore, he was always addressed by the *New York Times* as 'Sir Rabindranath'.

Everyone knew it, except the gullible public of India, and even today there is a well educated class in India, which believes that Rabindranath had actually returned the Knighthood.

Immediately after the massacre at Jallianwala Bagh, there was a demand from all over India to build a befitting memorial at Amritsar, but when the Congress lent support to it, Tagore opposed it, saying: "Let those, who wish to, try to burden the minds of future with stones, carrying the black memory of wrongs and their anger, but let us bequeath to the generations to come, memorials of that only which we can revere, ...".[63] The opposition was poetic, but gave a welcome relief to the British administration which at that time was under great pressure, both in India and England. Today a graceful memorial— built without any support form Tagore— stands at Jallianwala Bagh.

Even after the massacre, Tagore had his loyalty intact for the British monarchy. The 1919 Congress session was held at Amritsar under the presidentship of Pt. Motilal Nehru. Tagore was not present there, but had sent a massage in the form of a poem, in which he counselled to have faith in the King of England.

> "...Our orphaned world is blind And Godless. Yet
> I can never believe that you are lost to us My King.
> Though our poverty is great and deep Our shame.
> You will work behind a veil of despair And in your own time.
> Open the gates of the impossible
> ...Dark ruins at your touch become like a bud"[64]

14

The Book Gitanjali

It was Awarded the Nobel Prize

When *Gitanjali* is seen, it becomes impossible to miss the small size of the book and exclaim: "This small book got the Nobel Prize". The original in Bengali was published in 1910, and the English translation, of 103 verses, on November 1, 1912, by India Society at London. There is an interesting story about the printing of *Gitanjali* by the India Society. The Macmillan Press had limited printing capacity and was overbooked. So, when William Rothenstein approached the press with the request to print *Gitanjali* within a month or so, he was refused and informed that the earliest date would be sometime in the month of March of the following year. Rothenstein was in a fix because the Swedish Nobel committee had a strictly enforced deadline of 1st February for accepting the nominations, and any nomination received after that date would have been ignored. As only a printed book can be submitted, Rothenstein had to plead with the India Society to publish *Gitanjali*, so that it could be sent before the deadline.

The next edition was brought out by Macmillan in March 1913, which still keeps it in print. The size of the book is small, and it has the thickness of 87 pages, including an eleven-page long introduction by W.B. Yeats. Though the thickness of a book can never be a criteria for determining its value, but if a book of 87 pages can be judged as a great work of literature, then why not another book of equal quality but having one page less, and why only one page and not ten or twenty pages less? How can only a few pages of literary creation ever be judged to deserve a prize like the Nobel Prize? *Gitanjali* literally means 'Song offerings', but the entire book has not a single song to offer, and whatever is there, is in prose form.

When on June 27, 1912, William Butler Yeats met Tagore, they were strangers, and neither of them had ever read a word written by either of them. Yet Yeats, after reading some 103 prose translations and not a word of the original poetry by Tagore, persuaded himself to declare that through his "...poetry the new Renaissance has been born",[65] in India.

W.B.Yeats has written a beautiful and long introduction for *Gitanjali*. He wrote "A few days ago I said to a distinguished Bengali doctor of Medicine ...though these prose translations from Rabindranath Tagore have stirred my blood as nothing has for years, I shall not know anything of his life." The Bengali doctor from Calcutta replied: "I read Rabindranath every day, to read one line of his to forget all the troubles of the world".[66] Yeats later on in his introduction predicts: " These verses will not lie in little well printed books upon ladies' tables, who turn the pages with indolent hands that they may sigh over a life without meaning, which is yet all they can know of life, or be carried about by students at the university to be laid aside when the work of life begins, but, as the generations pass, travellers will hum them on the highway and men rowing upon rivers. Lovers, while they await one another, shall find, in murmuring them, this love of God a magic gulf wherein their own more bitter passion may bathe and renew its youth".[67] Since then, several generations have passed, without any being aware of Yeats' predictions. Probably it was Rothenstein's the persistent persuasion which persuaded Yeats to write such an introduction. Moreover, Yeats also possessed a poetic licence to write, whatever he fancied, for he had declared: "Inaccuracies don't worry me, so long as the phrase is beautiful."[68] Probably it was the beauty of the phrase, which inspired him to write in the introduction: "I have carried the manuscript of these translations about with me for days, reading it in railway trains, or on the top of omnibuses and in restaurants, and I have often had to close it lest some stranger would see how much it moved me." [69] Omnibuses were horse-drawn public carriages with solid rubber tyres; it was difficult to even sit steadily in these carriages, not to mention reading a handwritten manuscript.

If it was the influence of Rothenstein; it waned, and if it was the poetic licence, Yeats corrected himself by writing in 1917 to Macmillan, Tagore's official publisher, "After 'Gitanjali' and 'The Gardener' and 'The Crescent Moon', and a couple of plays and 'Sadhana', nothing more should have been published, except the long autobiography... These later poems are drowning his reputation"[70]. Advancing age makes a man blunt. This was exactly what happened to Yeats. Just four years before his death, in a letter of May 1935, he wrote to Rothenstein: "Damn Tagore. We got out three good books, Sturge Moore and I, and then, because he thought it was more important to see and know English than to be a great poet". As if passing his last judgement on Rabindranath, he added: "He brought out sentimental rubbish and wrecked his reputation. Tagore does not know English."[71]

Maturing age not only makes a man forthright but also more truthful. The letter of Yeats was written in May and as if agreeing with it, the very next month in June of

1935, the ageing Tagore candidly confessed in a letter to Sturge Moore, the Englishman, who had proposed *Gitanjali* to the Swedish Academy for the Nobel Prize.

> "I am no longer young, and I have had ample time to realise the futility of going out of one's own natural sphere for winning recognition. Languages are jealous sovereigns and passports are rarely allowed for travellers to cross their strictly guarded boundaries. What is the use of awkwardly knocking my head against their prohibitions". About the translated literature, the opinion of the mature Rabindranath was: "Translations, however clever, can only transfigure dancing into acrobatic tricks, in most cases playing treason against the majesty of the original. I often imagine apes to be an attempt by the devil of a translator to render human form in the mould of his own outlandish idiom"[72]

True, poetry when translated, especially from an Oriental to a western language, loses its beauty and poise. The difference in the cultural outlook is so great that the translated work turns out to be a mere black and white shadow of the multicoloured original. When Tagore wrote the latter to Sturge Moore, he had the wisdom of 75 years, and if the mature poet had such an opinion about the translated works, then the decision of the Swedish Academy, to select the translated Gitanjali for the prize, seems unusual.

In an experiment four prose verses were selected:

1

I have had my invitation to this world's festival, and thus my life has been blessed. My eyes have seen and my ears have heard.

It was my part at this feast to play upon my instrument, and I have done all I could.

Now, I ask, "Has the time come at last when I may go in and see thy face and offer thee my silent salutation?"

2

I came alone to this world. I started my journey to meet someone. He was playing the flute of life. I came upon mountains, it was the music which made me climb.

I came upon deserts, it was the music which kept me walking. I came upon rivers, it was the music which made me cross.

Now I come to the end of the journey. Where is the flute? Where is the music? Mercy! Play it for I have to travel a step further.

3

Clouds have had made dark night more dark. I see no light. How shall I find my way?

Darkness is deep and the journey long. Shall I be lost forever? Suddenly I see a flicker of light. Instantly I know it was you, my master. It was the flicker of thou kindness.

It was far away and I shall stumble many times. But I fear not injuries or the long journey.

With thou rays of kindness I shall reach you, my master.

4

He came and sat by my side but I woke not, what a cursed sleep it was, O miserable me!

He came when the night was still; he had his harp in his hand, and my dreams became resonant with its melodies.

Alas, why are my nights all thus lost? Ah, why do I ever miss his sight whose breath touches my sleep?

Many were asked to differentiate between these, but none could. Out of these four verses, two are from *Gitanjali*, and the other two are penned by a first time writer, without help from any quarter.[73]

It was my part at this feast to play upon my instrument, and I have done all I could.

Now, I ask, "Has the time come at last when I may go in and see thy face and offer thee my silent salutation?"

2

I came alone to this world. I started my journey to meet someone. He was playing the flute of life. I came upon mountains; it was the music which made me climb.

I came upon deserts; it was the music which kept me walking. I came upon rivers; it was the music which made me cross.

Now I am at the end of the journey. Where is the flute? Where is the music? Alas, neither it nor I have to travel [illegible]

3

Clouds have had made dark night more dark. I see no light. How shall I find my way?

Darkness is deep and the journey long. Shall I be lost forever? Suddenly I see a flicker of light. Instantly I knew it was you, my master. It was the flicker of thou kindness.

It was far away and I shall stumble many times. But I fear not injuries or the long journey.

With thou rays of kindness I shall reach you, my master.

4

He came and sat by my side but I woke not. What a cursed sleep it was, O miserable me!

He came when the night was still; he had his harp in his hand, and my dreams became resonant with its melodies.

Alas, why are my nights all thus lost? Ah, why do I ever miss his sight whose breath touches my sleep?

Many were asked to differentiate between these, but none could. Out of these four verses, two are from Gitanjali, and the other two are penned by a first time writer, without help from any quarter.

15

The Nobel Prize

A Few facts

In the 19th century, Alfred Nobel, a Swedish chemist, invented dynamite and this substance turned out to be the most destructive material ever possessed by man.

A thick yellowish oily liquid, nitroglycerine— nitro for short—was known to chemists for years. It was extremely unstable, and a mere splash while handling, or a sudden jerk while moving, was enough to cause a violent explosion. While handling this dreadful oil, many lost limbs and a few, even their lives. Alfred Nobel, a chemist, observed that Kieselguhr, a porous German earth found naturally, can retain considerable quantity of nitro, which after being absorbed into the earth, was no longer a free-flowing fluid, and could not explode easily. Kieselguhr had tamed the furious beast nitro, by imprisoning it in its millions of porous cells. Alfred Nobel further improved it by adding wood pulp and sodium nitrate, and it was christened Straight dynamite, the first of the many varieties of dynamite. Unable to splash, the unsafe had become safe and now nitro could be transported as dynamite from the chemical plant to the site of use, without the risk of an explosion.

The destruction caused by the dynamite was unparalleled in the entire history of mankind. Dynamite brought destruction to the world and riches for Nobel, and the more dynamite destroyed, the richer he became, but the rich Nobel was not a happy Nobel. Along with the global destruction, dynamite had also destroyed a part of Nobel. Tormented by self-guilt, he decided to bequeath his vast wealth amassed by destruction, for construction. In his will, Alfred directed that the income from his estate should be used for the distribution of five prizes, to be given annually, for outstanding work done in the field of physics, chemistry, medicine, literature and for the most effective work done in the interest of international peace. Through the peace prize, he had attempted to mitigate the destruction caused by dynamite.

When Nobel wrote his will, Sweden and Norway were in a common union, which lasted up to 1905. Significantly, Nobel entrusted not a Swedish but a Norwegian institute for awarding the prize for peace. Norway selects the prize winner for international peace and the remaining four, by different Swedish institutions in Stockholm—the capital of Sweden. Nobel died in 1896, but the distribution of the prizes could begin only from 1901, because of some legal lacunae in the will. A sixth prize was added in 1969 by the Bank of Sweden for excellence in economic sciences, which was funded by the Bank.

The Royal Swedish Academy of Sciences selects the winning candidates for the prizes of physics, chemistry and economics, and Karolinska Institute, a premier medical centre, has the responsibility to find the person, who has made an outstanding contribution in the field of medicine or physiology. The Swedish Academy chooses a writer for the most distinguished literary work. Alfred had willed that the literary work selected should be 'idealistic in nature'. Only the work which has appeared in print is considered, and as stipulated in the Nobel-will, the prize could be given only to a living person and never posthumously. All the academies are situated at the capital of Sweden, Stockholm. Storting (Parliament) of Norway elects a Norwegian Nobel Committee, which selects the winner for the international peace prize, to be awarded at an impressive ceremony in Oslo, the capital of Norway. Alfred Nobel imposed such conditions in his will that Sweden had a minimal role to play in the selection of the peace prize. After the dissolution of her union with Norway in 1905, Sweden ceased to have any role in it.

No academy ever generated more controversies than the Swedish Academy, responsible for selecting the prize winner for literature, and two causes were mainly responsible for it. The lesser one was that no one could propose a writer, unless he himself belonged to an exclusive group, eligibility for which was decided by the Academy. William Rothenstein had to seek Thomas Sturge Moore, a fellow of the Royal Society of Literature, for proposing *Gitanjali*. It is understandable, if the name of every writer is proposed then the Academy will cease to meaningfully function, but by licensing only a few select groups, some with vested interests, many great writers were never nominated. Anton Chekhov died in 1904 and for three years was eligible for nomination, but his name was never proposed. Leo Tolstoy was proposed once only in 1902. He lived till 1910 and the name of this great writer could have been considered for the prize on eight more occasions, but every year he was ignored, so were Emile Zola and Mark Twain. The second and more relevant reason was the way the Swedish Academy selected the winner. In theory the Academy was an autonomous body and its members were independent and free to select a Nobel Prize winner, but in fact the autonomy of the Academy, in its early years, was a myth.

The Swedish Academy was founded in the Stockholm stock exchange building, on April 5, 1786, by the King of

Sweden, Gustaf III, on the pattern of the French Academy in Paris. The French had forty members and the King initially intended to appoint half of these in the Swedish Academy, but he, superstitiously, believed in the number eighteen and so eighteen were installed. The number of members in the Academy is still the same, where once appointed they serve for life. The founder members were selected by the King himself. When the Academy loses one of its members, a new one is elected by a secret ballot and his name is submitted to the King, the patron of the Academy, for approval. If the Academy ever overlooked the loyalty of the new aspirant, the King could veto, and with this power, the King would always keep the Academy faithful to him. The King also wrote the statute of the Academy, which resembled the rules of the French Academy. In the early years, the members of the Academy were mainly government officials, jurists, religionists, philologists, historians and linguists. Writers—who understand literature and appreciate the new trends—were also there, but in a minority. Some time, during the second quarter of 20th century, the number of writers increased and only towards the end of the century, were they in a majority. The Academy was and still is a predominątely male dominated place. In its entire history of 220 years, only six females have so far been elected as the members. Selma Lagerlof elected in 1914, after a period of 128 years, was the first lady member of the Academy.

The members of the Academy elect one of themselves, for the post of the Permanent Secretary. Elected for life — by a recent rule he retires at the age of 70, unless the Academy decides otherwise — the Secretary is the most important functionary of the Academy. He is the spokesman of the Academy, keeps the minutes, calls meetings and generally acts as the chief executive of the Academy. He also keeps a close liaison with the Patron of the Academy, the King of Sweden. Many of the Pėrmanent Secretaries became so powerful that it was impossible for the members to ignore them. One of them was Carl David'af Wirsen, who, elected in 1884, was very close to the King, whose dislike for the Russians was well known. So great was the influence of Wirsen, that in 1902, when Leo Tolstoy, a Russian, was nominated along with Theodor Mommsen and Herbert Spencer, he strongly denounced Tolstoy and almost single-handedly convinced the Academy to vote in favour of Mommsen. The rejection of Tolstoy shocked the literary world, and in Sweden alone, some fifty writers and artists castigated the Academy and moved a petition favouring Tolstoy. Nothing happened. The influential Permanent Secretary remained where he was, and Tolstoy was never selected for the prize. Such was the power of the Permanent Secretary.

In 1913, Wirsen was succeeded by Erik Axel Karlfeldt, who too was close to the King, and had the additional qualification of being a poet. During the very first year of his tenure, Rabindranath was nominated along with Thomas Hardy, a 73-year-old English novelist and a poet, who was another serious contender for the prize. While Hardy had authored an impressive number of books, only three works — *Gitanjali, Gardner* and *Sadhana* — by Tagore were available. Erik was a poet and when, as a poet, he passionately praised and vouched for the fine quality of the poems written by Rabindranath, the majority of the Academy—who knew little about poetry—decided to cast their votes in favour of Rabindranath, and he was elected.

The eighteen members of the Academy were experienced and knowledgeable men of great integrity. They were the best that Sweden could offer. Nevertheless they were humans with their likes and dislikes, prejudices, vanities and above all, fears. Like other mortals, they too could be influenced, and perhaps intimidated. They were knowledgeable in one field and totally ignorant in another. In 1913, the writers in the Academy were in a distinct minority, and the rest—who formed the majority— had little or no experience of contemporary literature, and could be made to like, or even dislike almost any writer, as Leo Tolstoy was.

The will had stipulated that the prize-winner must have an "idealistic tendency" and this edict of Alfred Nobel was used or ignored, at the convenience of those who mattered in the Academy. It was used when they wanted to award the prize to Tagore, and ignored in the case of chest-beating war-monger Churchill, who had no relation with the literature of 'idealistic tendency'. As a matter of fact, the Academy under pressure could ignore almost any rule. In 1931, the Swedish Academy broke its most inflexible rule and awarded the Nobel Prize to a dead man. Erik, the Permanent Secretary of the Academy had died— during his tenure Tagore was selected for the Prize— without leaving enough assets for his widow and daughters. So the Academy gave him the prize money. Under the rule, the name of a dead man could never be considered for an award. Erik Axel Karlfeldt had died on April 8, 1931, months before his name was considered and almost seven months before the final selection, still he was posthumously selected and awarded the 1931 Nobel Prize for literature. It is not known whether the award to the dead Erik was a reward for his loyalty and obedience to Gustaf or if it was the arm twisting of the Academy by Erik's widow. What the reason was, no one can ever be sure, except that without a royal assent, it would not have been possible to make such a flagrant violation of the rule book.

Forty-nine-year old Gustaf V, who in 1907 was anointed as the King of Sweden, had inherited a prosperous nation but a weak army. Only two years earlier in 1905, Norway had broken her 90-year-old union with Sweden. The union was not only important but immensely beneficial to her because Norway had a long shore line and easy access to the sea, which was open even during winter. Devoid of the union, Sweden was reduced to the status of a small nation without year round access to the sea. Though there was no clear evidence, but many believed that bad big brother Russia, their next door neighbour, was behind the break. Sweden in the past had lost Finland to Russia in 1809. Although it was 100 years ago, but Finland was still the property of the Czar of Russia. Humiliation had lingered in the memory of Sweden.

Come September and Stockholm becomes the centre of hectic activities of the Royal Swedish Academy of Sciences, Karolinska Institute and the Swedish Academy. After receiving the last nomination up to February 1 of the year, various boards become busy, in shifting the large volume of the nominations. The Swedish Academy appoints a four-member board to go through all the nominations, and in April it presents to the Academy, for approval, a preliminary list of selected candidates. The Academy may further reduce the list, and then the selected books of these candidates are sent to all the members of the Academy. All through summer, the eighteen members read and re-read these books. In September, for the first time, they all meet formally to discus, what they had read during the summer months. At this meeting they also speak in favour of or against the various writers, during which the list is further reduced to just a few. These are the final candidates. In November, the members of the Academy meet again, this time in camera—where no outsider is allowed through the locked doors—and debate, generally for several hours, and in the end ballots are passed. The winner must get more than half of the votes cast; otherwise the process is repeated until a winner is selected. His name is then forwarded to the King, the patron of the Academy, and after his approval, the name is publicly announced for the 23 carat gold medallion and the accompanying fat cheque, to be given after a week-long extravaganza, in the late afternoon of 10th Dec., the anniversary of the death of Alfred Nobel.

The September of 1913 was no different. The usual activities had started in Stockholm, but King Gustaf was restless. Crown Princess Margaret had gone to London to meet her parents, and recently had come back with the regards from her parents and greetings from her cousin, King George. She also informed that all of them were expecting a war any time in near future, and it was this news which had made Gustaf restless. He himself could hear, loudly and clearly, the war rumblings coming from the direction of his neighbour, Germany. There were only a few shallow miles of Baltic Sea as his sole protection from the mighty eagle of the second Reich. He had decided to remain neutral in case there was a war, as his small army was no match for the military might of his neighbours. But in case Gustaf was forced to join the war, how Sweden would avoid the sure destruction? Even his experienced and trusted ministers had not been able to provide an acceptable answer to this question. He never knew the gold crown on his head was so heavy.

Though he had decided to seek help for sparring Sweden from the ravages of war, but knew that no favours could be expected without a price. He was prepared to trade, but did not know what to offer, as his small country had almost nothing to proffer, perhaps with the exception of a piece or two of the Nobel gold.

After a few months the Word War started, resulting in terrible destruction all over Europe, but Sweden was spared and remained unharmed.

Thousands of kilometres away, there was another king who too, for the first time, was finding his gold crown heavy. He was the King of England, George V.

His elder brother, Prince Edward was to be crowned as the King of England, but by a stroke of bad luck he developed pneumonia, which was a grave and usually fatal disease in that era, without antibiotics. Edward died, and George not only got the throne, his brother was to occupy, but also the girl, whom Edward was to marry. George married the German princess, Mary of Teck, who was engaged to his brother. By the smiling lady luck, George was gifted with a vast empire and a beautiful maid, both initially intended for his elder brother. Both were taken seriously.

George fathered six children:
Edward in 1894
George in 1895
Mary in 1897
Henry in 1900 and
John in 1905

Thus, George was fathering a child with the regularity of a few years, but after 1905, this forty-year young future King of England probably became so engaged in learning the state craft—for which he was extensively coached by the masters of the art—that he devoted all his energies in mastering it, and at the young age of 40, stopped fathering any further. It seems that all his time was now only for his newly acquired mistress, the British Empire.

George was a devoted lover, and he was determined to keep his new mistress happy and in sound health. He knew that Britain was a world power only as long as she had her empire, particularly India. In his plan, India was so important that he became the first and incidentally the only king, who with his own eyes would see the vast Indian wealth and the immense manpower. He was aware that the 250 million Indians were ruled by a mere handful of English, whose number was never more than 90,000. He also knew that the rule of India could continue only as long as Britain was able to maintain a facade of a benevolent ruler. India had almost willingly accepted the rule of Britain, and at this hour of want, her cooperation was essential for the empire. The need of it was always there, but with the possibility of a European war, it was acutely felt. In the event of the war, he wanted Indians to contribute their wealth, as well as their lives, to safeguard the interests of Britain.

The Swedish constitution was framed anew in 1809, and gave the King vast executive powers, which remained with him till the end of the First World War. In 1917, when many monarchies were vanishing, he was spared but his powers were greatly curtailed. In 1975 the Swedish constitution was again amended and the King was reduced to a ceremonial head of the state. Unlike the king of today, Gustaf in 1913 had vast power, prestige and influence. It may be called flattery or regard for the King, but it was impossible for any Nobel body to ignore the wish of their King. Gustaf had a special dislike for Russia, while Germany was his favourite nation. Russians were regarded as rustic, uncultured and non-Europeans, while Germans were accepted as advanced and intellectual people, and this reflected in the selection of the Nobel Prize winners. For the first fifty years, each year a German got a Nobel Prize. Their total was forty-five, because during the intervening two World Wars, many prizes were not awarded. During the same period, in all the categories, Russians were given only three prizes. Only after the Allied forces defeated Germany in the Second World War, the trend changed.

A vast country, Russia was the birthplace of many great writers, yet for decades, none of them were found fit for the Nobel Prize. Most notable was Leo Tolstoy, author of the superb literary masterpiece *War and Peace.* Actually by not selecting Tolstoy, the Swedish Academy only tarnished its own reputation. There was also the master story writer, Anton Chekhov, who was capable of bringing human characters to life by the deft strokes of his pen. He too was ignored, so was Maxim Gorky. The Swedish Academy kept ignoring the Russian writers for as many as 65 years when at last the first actual Nobel Prize for literature was given to Mikhail Sholokhov for his novels.

In between, two sham Nobel prizes were given to the writers from Russia. The first was given to 63-year-old Ivan Bunin in 1933, whose sole qualification was writing about the miseries of Russian life. Ivan had exiled himself from Russia in 1919, immediately after the Bolshevik revolution and settled down in France, and only when it was clear that he had no intention of returning to Russia — by then he had been living in France for 14 years — Ivan became the first Russian to receive the Nobel Prize. The greatly controversial second Nobel Prize was given to Boris Pasternak for his work on sufferings and disorders in Russia. He was selected in 1958, for his book *Dr. Zhivago*. The writers' community of Soviet Russia was shocked, and realising the truth, Boris refused to accept the prize.

English Princess Marries Swedish Prince

Margaret Victoria Charlotte Augusta Norah was quite a mouthful of a name. Her father, Prince Arthur, was the son of Queen Victoria and her mother, Princess Margaret, was from a Prussian (present-day Germany) Royal House. As her parents had to accommodate the names from both the royal families, she was given such a long name; otherwise she was simply called Margaret. By the time Margaret crossed her teens, she metamorphosed into a ravishing beauty. A long slender body and a finely chiselled face made her, the niece of the king of England, Edward VII, the heart throb of many kings and crown princes of Europe.

Queen Victoria of Great Britain was the fountainhead of a defective bloodline. As a result, many of the English princesses, who were her daughters and granddaughters, carried a mysterious hidden disease. They never suffered, and a female child born to them too always remained healthy, but many of their male children suffered from a strange ailment, in which the bleeding, due to any injury, would not stop easily. Unknown at that time, they were suffering from Haemophilia, a serious blood disorder in which the disease is introduced by the mother only in her male children. Tests to detect the disorder were still not available. Moreover the doctors had not linked the disease to the mother. As a result, all over Europe, English princesses were still in great demand.

In the first month of 1905, Margaret in the company of her parents and a younger sister went to Portugal, with the aim to find suitable matches for herself and her sister. The Portuguese desired that either of the English princesses should be their future queen. The English party was warmly received by King Carlos and Queen Amelia of Portugal, and their sons, Crown Prince Luis and Prince Maroel, made spirited efforts to win the hearts of the English princesses, but all they could get were polite smiles and firm nos. Next on their itinerary was Spain, who also was in intensive search for a blue blooded princess for her bachelor King Alfonso XIII, but the proposal from the Spanish king too, was politely declined.

The girls had rejected a king, a crown prince and a prince. As a result their parents were visibly disappointed, and the only thing they now wanted was to head home and mount a search from there, to find suitable bridegrooms for their haughty daughters. But fate had destined differently, as Margaret and her younger sister Patricia were both eager to see the great Pyramids, the English party moved on to Egypt. Princess Margaret saw the Pyramids, but there she also met a young man whom she found far more attractive than the deaf and dumb stone Pyramids. That young man was tall, dark haired and danced excellently, and before the inexperienced young English princess could realise, she was under the spell of this enticing enchanter. It was truly love at first sight. The predictable proposal came at a dinner party and Margaret said 'Yes' before the long worded proposal could be finished by that handsome young man.

That man, Prince Gustaf Adolf of Sweden, was the grandson of the Swedish King Oscar II and son of crown prince Gustaf. Under his charisma, Margaret overlooked the fact that her prince charming was a year younger and wore glasses. They got married, with all the royal pomp and show, on June 15, 1905 at St. George's Chapel, situated within Windsor castle.

Time passed in Sweden. Oscar died and his son Gustaf was installed in 1907, as the King of Sweden, who assumed the name of King Gustaf V. His son, Gustaf Adolf, was now the crown prince and his wife, Margaret, the crown princess.

Time passed in Britain too. The potbellied, indiscriminate and compulsive eater Edward VII, the King of England, died of stomach infection in 1910. Now, George V was the King of England and Margaret, his first cousin, the crown princess of Sweden. With this relationship, George had a direct link with the royal household of Sweden and the potential to influence the Nobel prize.

King George V

In the Britain of today, the King and Queen can be found at two places, first in a pack of cards and second in Buckingham Palace. Both can be checkmated, for there is an ace for the king in the pack, and a Prime Minister to rule over the one, living in the palace. Both have equal powers, for once out of the pack, its King and Queen are as powerless as the live are, when they step out of Buckingham Palace., but days were different when Edward's second son was given the reins of the British Empire. George V not only had real power but was a king with a difference.

He was lucky—His elder brother, Prince Edward was heir apparent to the British throne, who was also engaged to a German beauty, Princess Mary. Everyone was very happy, for Edward was a bright man and everyone expected him to be an able king, but fate had destined differently. Edward fell ill in 1892, and died of pneumonia. Lucky George got both, the throne as well as the girl.

He was shrewd—When in 1911, the upper house, the House of Lords, with a conservative majority tried to stop an Act moved in the parliament by the liberals, where they were in a majority; George shrewdly intervened and threatened to invoke his royal powers to create enough new liberal peers in the House of Lords to remove the conservative majority. Faced with a situation, in which the House of Lords would have a permanent liberal majority, the conservatives agreed.

He was dedicated—George married the charming Princess Mary in 1893, and the very next year their first child was born, to be followed by five more in succession. George was a young man of 40 when he was father for the last time, because from that time onward he dedicated himself only to the affairs of the Empire, probably with no time of his own left.

He was industrious—It is a part of recorded history that the King visited the battlefields for over 450 times to personally meet the troops, during the four-year span of the First World War. He went to hospitals over 300 times, to enquire about the wounded, and often he visited daily for weeks together. While on a visit to a war front in France in 1915, he fell from his horse and sustained a fracture of the pelvic bone. However, after resting for only a few days, he was back again to meet his troops.

Sentiments never moved him—Ancestors of the British royal family were linked to Germany, from where they had adopted a German name 'Saxe-Coburg-Gotha' for the British royal family. They had many close relations there, and even the wife of George, Mary of Teck, was a German princess, but when Britain was at war with Germany during the First World War, there were strong anti-German feelings in Britain, so George decided to change the name of the royal family. Sentiment and tradition bound royal families opposed it, but George overruled all of them, and changed the royal family's name to 'House of Windsor'.

Again in 1917, George took the callous and cruel decision to decline asylum to Czar Nicholas II, his wife and their five children, even though the Czarina was his first cousin, and the defective British blood was the main cause of their troubles. The story of the British blood, which has left a long trail of sad stories over all of Europe, is like this:

Every human being has exactly 23 pairs of chromosomes in each cell of the body, and out of these, one particular pair is called sex chromosomes, because they are responsible for deciding the sex of the human body. They are symbolised by X and Y letters. If both are X (XX), the human body is female and if one is X and another Y (XY), the body is male. Genes present in the X chromosome are responsible for the production of a compound, known as factor VIII, which is essential to stop bleeding, and if this factor is absent, the human body will bleed profusely. This condition is called haemophilia. Because both the X chromosomes have similar and almost equal ability to cause the production of factor VIII, only males suffer from haemophilia, for they have only one X chromosome and if it is defective, there will be deficiency of the factor VIII. On the other hand, females almost always never suffer, for they have two X chromosomes, and if one is defective, the other can still maintain the production of factor VIII to keep that female body healthy. In bygone times there was no remedy for haemophilia and males with defective X chromosomes eventually died of excessive bleeding, while females with defective X chromosome remained healthy, but kept on passing the defective chromosome to the next generation. A male with defective X chromosome was also capable of passing the defect to the next generation. But his male offspring were always normal because they got their X chromosome form their mother. His daughters invariably inherited the defect, because their X chromosome, contributed by their father, was always defective. All the daughters, with defective chromosome, though never suffered but were capable of passing the disease to their male progeny. In the terminology of medical men, they are called carriers, because without suffering they carry the disease to their child.

The severity of haemophilia depends upon the degree of defect in the X chromosome. A male can expect to live a near normal life with as little as 30 per cent production of factor VIII, which is possible with minor defects in the X chromosome, as we will see was probably the case with John Conroy. With grossly defective X chromosome the production of factor VIII may fall as low as 4 to 5 per cent, resulting in a full blown picture of classical haemophilia, as we will find on the following pages was the case with Czarevitch Alexis.

There was no previous haemophilic in the family line of Queen Victoria, and she was the first one in the British royal family, to be born with the defective chromosome. Medical investigations revealed that many in the royal family suffered from mental instability. Grandfather of Victoria, King George III, was so mentally ill that by 1810, he became totally unfit to perform the duties of the king, and his son,

George, was made regent to carry on the royal obligations, who after the death of George III was coronated to become King George IV. As time passed George IV, uncle of Victoria, also became mentally unstable and died in 1830 as a recluse. Victoria's second uncle, William IV was also, by the time he became old, mentally unbalanced. The cases of madness in the royal family were attributed to Porphyria, a genetically transmittable disease, which can pass from one generation to the next, by the genes. From Queen Victoria onwards, none of her descendants showed Porphyria, and cases of mental instability abruptly ceased to occur in the British royal family. Instead, cases of haemophilia surfaced, and Prince Leopold, son of Queen Victoria, was the first victim of it. He died of excessive bleeding at the young age of 31 years.

How the grandmother of King George V, the Queen of England, could become a carrier of haemophilia, a trait which almost always can only be inherited from parents and the parents can have it only from their parents and so on, is a mystery. On medical scrutiny, it was found that none of her ancestors for 17 generations ever suffered form haemophilia. Then, from where did Victoria have the defective genes in her X chromosome?

Victoria's father, Edward the Duke of Kent, was the son of George III, the King of England, who had four sons. Edward, the youngest, was an easy going and fun loving spoiled brat. After the king's death, the eldest brother of Edward was coronated, who is known in history as King George IV. In due course the King was blessed with a daughter so charming that she was named Charlotte. She was the future queen of England.

One brother of the King died and the surviving two, William and Edward, adopted the path of carnal pleasure. Their way of life, with so many concubines and mistresses, was not possible with lawfully wedded wives, so they never married. Time passed on happily, rather too happily for both of them, as riches from the royal treasury were freely available to them, but in the world nothing is free and their pleasures were also not free. All along they kept paying with the taxpayers' money and their own health, and by the time they had celebrated their 50th birthday, both of them were like a pair of worn-out muzzle loading muskets of their time, which had been charged and fired so often that they ceased to fire, and if with great care and much coaxing ever fired, the bullet never went straight and rarely found the target.

Towards the end of the second decade of the 19th century, duo brothers, William and Edward, were living a blissfully contented life, unmindful of the fact that the candles of their lives were burning from both ends. And nothing would have changed, had a tragic incident not occurred in the royal household. Two years before the decade would end, two lives in the British royal family ended. In 1818, Princess Charlotte and her newborn died. It was a case of obstructed labour, during which the dead baby was forcefully pulled out. The mother was mortally injured and bled to death.

Britain was stunned, as there was no heir to the throne from the next generation. The king's only child had died. Although his brother William had at least ten children from his known mistress, an actress called Dorothy Jordon, and several more from many unknown concubines. But all of them were illegitimate and none could be made the King. The youngest brother Edward was also living an unrestrained colourful life with many mistresses from the demimonde of London and had many issues. However, all of them, nearly one dozen, were illegitimate and none could ever occupy the British throne.

Princess Charlotte's death paved the way for William to become the next king of England, and if Edward could outlive William, then one day he too could be a crowned king. It was greed for the British throne which overpowered them, and both the sinners vowed, never to sin again. Abandoning their all known and unknown mistresses, both promised to marry and provide an acceptable and legitimate heir for the throne, but both, long back worn out muskets of over fifty years vintage, were not sure of their firing powers. It seems that William, a confirmed procreator of at least ten illegitimates, was more confident, and within days of Princess Charlotte's death, he married a virgin named Adelaide, who was the daughter of the Duke of Saxe Coburg, but he never could keep his young wife satisfied. He was well over fifty, and his by now weak sperms produced one after another, two unhealthy children, who died in infancy. After the death of the second child, his discontented wife left, never to return.

With his failing health, Edward was less confident, and he selected a well-trodden path. His choice was a widow, who was twenty years younger. This voluptuous lady, Victoria Maria Louisa, was the sister of King Leopold of Belgium. She was married to a minor German prince, who years ago had died in a war. As a widow, she was leading a frugal life in the small principality of her dead husband, so when Edward proposed to Maria, she eagerly accepted in anticipation of an opulent and easy life in the prosperous British royal court.

Thirty-one years old and a vivacious beauty form Germany married fifty-one year old and ailing Edward in 1818. Many had doubts about the virility of the old Edward, as he was permanently ill and his health was falling with every passing day. But within days of the marriage, Maria was pregnant, and Victoria, the future queen of England, was in her womb. Sick Edward died, one year and five months after the day Louisa began to carry the growing foetus, inside her.

The swiftness with which Maria got pregnant made many suspicious, but before rumours could permanently harm the claim of their unborn child, the couple shifted to the principality of Maria's dead first husband. The life in that remote German town was harsh, but at least their unborn in the womb was hundreds of miles away from the damaging rumours. They hurried back to Britain, just a few days before Maria was to give birth on May 24, 1819, to a female child, the future heir to the throne of England. The child was named Alexandria Victoria. Eight months after her birth, Edward the Duke of Kent died. When he died on January 23, 1820, he was unaware that one day his baby girl would be the most powerful monarch of the world. He was also unaware that his daughter was carrying a defective X chromosome, destined to play havoc with the history of Europe.

Even before Victoria could come out from the womb, it was rumoured that the Duke of Kent was not her father, and the reason behind it was his ill health. During the last several years, when he was comparatively healthier and had the company of several mistresses, he had not been able to father a single child. Now when more years had been added to his age, how the old duke could suddenly become potent enough to make Maria Louisa pregnant within weeks of their nuptial knot? In fact he was so ill that he died 17 months after the night Maria got pregnant. There was one more fact, and at that time no one was aware of it. Baby Victoria was carrying a haemophilic chromosome, even though none of her ancestors— as revealed by careful medical investigations— for 17 generations had ever suffered from haemophilia.

According to circulating rumours, Edward was not fit for procreation. For argument's sake even if he was, he definitely was not a haemophilic. But if Edward was not that man, then who else was responsible for making Maria pregnant with his defective sperm? The name suspected most was that of an Irishman, John Conroy. He was an ambitious officer in the British royal court. The suspicion becomes stronger, when history reveals that widow Maria had and continued to have intimately close relations with Conroy, even after her second husband's death.

The growing Victoria may have seen and heard when Conroy and Maria were together and a little careless. She probably had an inkling of the clandestine affair, for as soon as she became the Queen of England in 1837, she permanently banished the dear friend of her mother, John Conroy, from the Royal Court and exiled her mother, Maria, to a set of apartments at the distal end of Buckingham Palace. Victoria also left strict instructions that her mother was never to be given access to the portion of the royal palace where she lived. On the basis of medical research and the fact that Maria Louisa was not a carrier of haemophilia, it can be surmised that the defective gene in the royal family of England was introduced by the lover of Louisa, and Victoria was the illegitimate daughter of John Conroy.

History at times likes to play jokes. In 1837, when the King of Britain, William IV died, he had at least ten children, but the British throne was denied to them because it was known to all that every one of them was illegitimate, while his niece Victoria was allowed the same throne, because no one knew that she was illegitimate, of course, with the sole exception of her mother, Maria. This illegitimate female was proclaimed the Empress of India and ruled over the British Empire for sixty-four years.

Victoria, as the queen mother, gave many magnificent gifts to her nine children and forty grandchildren, but the gift that history remembers most was the gift of the bad British blood. Her daughters and granddaughters carried the defective blood as their marriage gift from Queen Victoria to the royal families of Spain, Germany and Russia.

When the granddaughter of Queen Victoria, princess Alix, married the Czar of Russia, along with many gifts, the gift of Bad British Blood from her grandmother Victoria was also carried to the royal household of Russia. This gift was to one day, change the history of Russia. Princess Alix was the daughter of Princess Alice and grand daughter of Queen Victoria. After her marriage to the Emperor of Russia, Czar Nicolas II, she was given the title of Czarina Empress Alexandra Feodorovna. During the first ten years of their marriage, the imperial couple had four issues and all of them were girls. According to an old rule, only a male child could be the future emperor of Russia. That long awaited heir to the Russian throne, Czarevitch Alexis, was born on August 12, 1904, alas, along with the gift of the defective British blood. He was a full blown haemophilic.

Any minor injury and the Czarevitch would bleed copiously. Each time he bled his mother felt like dying of guilt, for she knew, she alone was responsible for transmitting the disease to her son. Time passed from one bleeding crisis to another and each time it looked as if the only heir to the Russian throne was going to bleed to death. One day, a rustic Russian named Rasputin came to the imperial court. Time and again, he was able to stop the bleeding by his mere presence, and this ability made him irreplaceable to the Czar. This hard drinking and morally loose mystic slowly started interfering in the working of the imperial court and the Czar had no option but to submit to the blackmail of Rasputin, because the very survival of his beloved son, the only heir of the Russian Empire, was in the hands of the illiterate monk. The hardships of the First World War (1914-1918) and staggering number of war casualties—17,00,000 Russians had died—made Czar unpopular, and the remaining goodwill was ruined by the misdeeds of the rascal, Rasputin. As a result, towards the end of the world war, there was considerable political unrest, and signs of an uprising against the regime of the Czar were clearly seen. Russia, under the leadership of Czar Nicolas II, had courageously fought the world war and the regime of the Czar would have regained its popularity, had there been no Rasputin to wreck its reputation, but the British Blood, brought to the imperial family of Russia by the granddaughter of Victoria, was responsible for the haemophilia of Czarevitch Alexis, and made the mighty Czar helpless before the ruinous misdeeds of Rasputin.

The Bolshevik revolution of 1917 forced Czar Nicolas to abdicate (March 1917). Fearing for the safety of herself and her family, Czarina Alix begged her cousin, the King of England, George V, for asylum in Britain— the country where her mother was born and her grandmother ruled for 64 years. George knew that the Czars had lost their empire, wealth, power and reputation, and giving asylum to this destitute family might prove to be a liability for the Royal House of Windsor, so asylum was denied. Czar Nicolas, his wife Czarina Alix, their four daughters Olga, Tatiana, Maril, Anastasia and son Alexis tried to escape the murderous mob of Bolshevik revolutionaries with the help of a few faithfuls, who were still loyal to them, but they could not. They were overtaken by armed Bolsheviks at Yekaterinburg, a small town at the border of Russia. Czars were overpowered and herded in a small room, where the bullets of the Bolsheviks killed them, one by one. All the seven bullet-ridden dead bodies of the Czars, who once were the mighty rulers of a vast empire, were dragged out and dumped, one over another, in a freshly dug mud pit. Such was the end of this tragic blood story.

In the First World War, the Czar was an ally of Britain, and together they fought against Germany. Russia had mobilised a great army of 1,20,00,000 soldiers, and Czar

Nicolas had personally directed the war manoeuvres, as the commander-in-chief of the Russian army. All along the days of war, King George had nothing else but praise for the tremendous contribution made by Nicolas, who also was his brother-in- law. Russia lost 17,00,000 soldiers in the war, and without the Russian help, it may have been impossible for Britain, to win in the war. But the highly valued friendship of Czar was forgotten the moment Nicolas was deposed in a coup by Bolshevik revolutionaries. Even the last minute mercy plea by Czarina Alix, his cousin, could not move the stony-hearted George V. He refused help, and all the Czars were ruthlessly killed.

He was calculating—When the nationalists in India were preparing the ground for Swaraj, King George was calculating his moves to checkmate them.

Addressing the delegates of the Congress at Surat in 1907, Bal Gangadhar Tilak had demanded Swaraj (self-rule) for India, he said: "We are not armed, and there is no necessity for arms either, we have a stronger weapon, political weapon in boycott". Even before Gandhi, the power of boycott was known to Tilak, who observed: "Every Englishman knows that they are a mere handful in this country and it is the business of everyone of them to befool you in believing that you are weak and they are strong." Tilak was aware that, at that time, there were merely 75,000 English troops and that was a small number for the 28,00,00,000 strong population of India, hence he advised: "We shall not assist them in fighting beyond the frontiers or outside India with Indian blood and money." He then asked a question: "Can you do that by your united efforts?" By answering the question himself: "If you can, you are free from tomorrow", he promised freedom to the people.

Tilak had hit the bull's eye, and the moderates, loyal to the crown, were mad with anger. They went on a rampage, and blood flowed in that Congress session. The English too were stunned. Tilak had found the truth about the might of the white men. The English were aware of the power of the boycott and knew that the success of Tilak and his ideas were sure to result in the end of the British Raj. Within days of his famous Surat speech, Tilak was arrested on June 24, 1908, on the charge of sedition, and was deported to Mandalay in Burma, where he was to remain behind the bars for six long years. Many of his nationalist friends were also jailed, and the remaining went under ground.

For the time being, white men were able to cap the volcano of discontent, but they were aware that these repressive steps would not help them forever and a lasting solution had to be found to perpetuate their Raj of India. Many suggestions were made, but all of them turned out to be as mediocre as their originators were, and were rejected. After many tedious discussions and several long meetings, one acceptable idea emerged. If they could find just a few, and if not a few, then only one or two natives, who could effectively influence the masses and remain loyal to the British cause, the people would not support boycott, and the Raj of India would remain safe.

In the past white men had tried Ram Mohun Roy. Initially he was successful and brought many under the influence of the English by propagating the Brahmo Samaj. But that pigmy at the end turned out to be a disaster and had to spend his last days and last pennies in untangling himself from the criminal cases of cheating in the British courts. They also tried the likes of Surendranath Banerjee, but he became such an obvious pet of the Raj that his fellow countrymen nicknamed him as Surrender Nath, and he lost his hold over the masses. The most effective weapon he could ever find to safeguard the interests of the Raj was a shoe, with the help of which he had tried to suppress the Swaraj demanding nationalists at the Surat session of the Congress.

The Empire tried to make him effective by the leftover morsels of power, but the purpose was not served, and the Indian masses remained unmoved.

The partition of Bengal had shocked the people and many youths of that important province of British India were becoming disloyal, but a solution to tame them was not in sight. First months passed, and then years, but the way out remained as elusive as ever. Before the first decade of the new century could end, it became clear that war in Europe was inevitable. The need to find that elusive solution was never more urgent, because in the event of a war, the British Empire was going to need Indian blood, as well as Indian money.

When the King came to Calcutta, and the whole situation was explained to him, he advised them to find an intellectual and not a politician. He was of the opinion that to be effective in a slave country like India, it was essential for a politician to oppose the regime. The King was right, because the masses followed only those who fought against the foreign rule, like Tilak. The ranks of moderates were full of political giants; still not a single popular leader could come out of it. The case with an intellectual was different, because his popularity was not tied down with any such constraint, for he can enter the hearts of the people in many subtle ways and influence their subconscious, without letting them ever know of it. The King held meetings with his trusted advisers, behind closed doors. What transpired in these can never be known, but we know that the King had come with the aim to garner greater support from India.

Rush of events was soon to overwhelm Rabindranath by surprise, for he was neither prepared nor forewarned. Many times he was even annoyed by the attention paid to him. Within days of the King's departure such events occurred, the like of which had never happened before in his entire past life of fifty years. The swiftness was indeed impressive.

Soon after the departure of the king:

Within days—Babu Rabindranath was felicitated at a grand function, ostensibly on his 50th birth anniversary.

Within weeks—Babu Rabindranath sailed to Britain with his book *Gitanjali,* with the aim to get the book published. When he sailed, the book was still not complete.

Within fortnights— An almost unknown, William Rothenstein on his own offered his unlimited and unsolicited services. He also got the book *Gitanjali* published.

Within months— A total stranger, W.B.Yeats, would start helping in the completion of the booklet. He also wrote a time consuming, long and flattering introduction for the book.

Another complete stranger, Thomas Moore, would come forward and recommended Rabindranath and his book *Gitanjali* for the Nobel prize, without really knowing the writer or his writings.

Within years—The Viceroy of India, Lord Harding, would order (October 1913) the Calcutta University to confer an honorary degree on Rabindranath, after overruling many objections.[75] The same year a Nobel Prize would be awarded to him (December 1913). A year and a half later, he would be knighted by the King himself. (June 1915)

Thus within a short span of three and a half years, starting from January1912 and ending on June 1915, an almost unknown Bengali poet, Babu Rabindranath became a national figure. He was now Dr. Rabindranath, Nobel

Laureate Rabindranath, Sir Rabindranath and above all Gurudev Rabindranath. So far he was Gurudev (respected teacher) of Shantiniketan School, but with the Nobel Prize he mesmerised the whole of Bengal, where he was now revered by all as Gurudev. He now had the power to influence the millions, and whoever was his friend was regarded as a friend of Bengal, or rather all of India. Thus the White man was perceived as the friend of India. Such was the influence of Rabindranath, and it overwhelmed almost all.

Six months and nineteen days after Rabindranath was awarded the Nobel Prize, the First World War started. The call of Tilak, "We shall not assist them...with Indian blood and money" was ignored. About 64,000 Indians lost their lives while fighting for the white men's cause in the white men's land. Indian money equivalent to 60,12,79,000 U.S. dollars was contributed to the war activities.[76] The Empire could also safely reduce the number of British soldiers in India from 75,000 to an all time low of 15,000, still there were no major disturbances in Bengal, during the period of the war. From India, fourteen lakh men were recruited for the fighting forces, together with four lakh non-combatants[77], with India paying from her coffers for their salary and upkeep.[51] Once again, Whiteman proved to be a cunning trader.

16

Vande Mataram

The Making of a National Anthem

The national anthem is the official song of a nation, intended to install pride and patriotism among the citizens of the country. Does the Indian national anthem 'Jana Gana Mana' have these qualities? No, it does not, because the song is full of self- pity and depicts the country in a state of 'stupor' and having 'dark evil dreams'. The country finally 'wakes up and bends her head' at the feet of a 'king of all kings', thus this song is fit only to be sung by slaves. Instead of pride and patriotism the song fills the hearts of the people with shame and remorse. If it is so, why was this song selected as the national anthem of free India?

The events that were responsible for making this song the national anthem of India occurred over a long period of time.

By the turn of the 20th century, Vande Mataram had become the star of the Indian eyes, the throb of the Indian hearts and the ruler of the Indian minds. No one in India could ignore it, and even Englishmen noticed it. They knew about the electrifying effect 'La Marseillaise' had on the French, in the year 1792, the year of the French Revolution. The British feared that one day, Vande Mataram might also become a La Marseillaise of India, and cause a revolution against them. So with all the might of the Empire, the English tried to suppress the spread of Vande Mataram, but the harder they tried, the more popular the song became. The Empire imposed punitive fines, people were beaten and even jailed for singing Vande Mataram, but none could douse the fire that was Vande Mataram.

When the upsurge of 1857 came, Bankim Chandra was a student at Presidency college of Calcutta. He was moved by the supreme sacrifice of his fellow compatriots, which they fearlessly offered in thousands, in an attempt to liberate their mother land. The war of independence had a lasting imprint on his young mind, and at that very moment he decided to serve his motherland, in whatever way possible for him in future.

For a Bengali graduate of that time, the only service that was available was with the government. He joined government service and in his own way served his countrymen, but he was not satisfied and took early retirement to devote all his time to writing a book, which would inspire the people for independence. His task was not easy, for India at that time was a slave country under the rule of Englishmen. Mere suspicion would have meant trouble and the book would have been confiscated, but he cleverly thought of a way out. Bengal of the 18th century was ruled by many arrogant and cruel Muslim landlords like Mir Kasim and Mir Jafar. At the same time, the terrible famine of Bengal in the year 1769-70 had starved to death over five million people, who mostly were uncared for Hindus. There were tens of thousands of Hindu families, where only one survivor was left. In most of the cases, that survivor was the strongest male member of the house, for the famine had killed all those who were weak. With no one in the family left to care for, these youths became sanyasis, wandering monks in saffron clothes. Many of them were educated and had an understanding of Hindu philosophy. These sanyasis preached to fight against injustice, and advised the poor starving masses to rebel against the tyranny of Muslims. This is known to history as the sanyasi rebellion, and it provided the desired background for the novel *Anand Math*. His actual aim was to prepare the people for an uprising against the English, and the Muslim backdrop was used only as a ploy to save his book from confiscation. Bankim Chandra wrote with great care, for he could not afford to let the British administration find fault with his novel. They never did.

The novel was serialised in 1880-82 in a Bengali magazine *Bangadarshan*, and in the year 1882, it came out in a book form. In the novel a young sanyasi Bhavananda meets a villager, who once was rich but was now reduced to penury. Both moan over the tragedy which had fallen over the people, and then, in a surge of emotions the sanyasi, belonging to a patriotic group known as Ananda Math, sings the song Vande Mataram. The song was actually written in November1875, almost five years before the novel *Ananda Math* was penned [167], but the song was so well integrated into the story, that none realised it was composed independently and years before the novel.

Vande Mataram

वन्दे मातरम्

||1||

सुजलां सुफलां मलयजशीतलाम्
शस्य श्यामलां मातरम्।
शुभ्रज्योत्स्नापुलकितयामिनीम्
फुल्लकुसमितद्रुमदलशोभिनीम्,
सुहासिनीं सुमधुर भाषिणीम्
सुखदां वरदां मातरम्।।

|| 2||

कोटि–कोटि कंठ कलकल–निनाद–कराले,
कोटि–कोटि भुजैर्धृत–खरकरवाले,

अबला केन मा एत बले।
बहुबलधारिणीं नमामि तारिणीम्
रिपुदलवारिणीं मातरम्।।

।।3।।

तुमि विद्या तुमि धर्म्म
तुमि हृदि तुमि मर्म्म
त्वं हि प्राणाः शरीरे
बाहुते तुमि मा शक्ति,
हृदये तुमि मा भक्ति,
तोमारई प्रतिमा गड़ि मंदिरे–मंदिरे मातरम्।।

।।4।।

त्वं हि दुर्गा दशप्रहरणधारिणीं
कमला कमलदल विहारिंणीं
वाणी विद्यादायिनी, नमामि त्वाम्
नमामि कमलां अमलां अतुलाम्
सुजलां सुफलां मातरम् ।।

।।5।।

वंदे मातरम्
श्यामलां सरलां सुस्मितां भूषिताम्
धरणीं भरणीं मातरम्।।

नोट : मूल गीत में 'सप्तकोटि–द्विसप्तकोटि' शब्द थे। 1937 के संशोधन कें अनुसार उन्हें 'त्रिशत कोटि–द्वित्रिशत कोटि' किया गया। 1950 से उन्हें भी बदलकर 'कोटि–कोटि' किया गया है।

That was more than one hundred and twenty-five years ago, but ever since the song has never failed to rouse the cravings for independence and fill the hearts with courage.

To make the song understandable to the English knowing people, Shri Aurbindo Ghosh translated the song into a beautiful English poem.

English Version:

(Rendered into English by Aurbindo Ghosh)

[1]
Mother, I bow to thee!
Rich with thy hurrying streams,
Bright with thy orchard gleams,
Cool with thy winds of delight,
Dark fields waving, Mother of might,
Mother free.

[2]
Glory of moonlight dreams,
Over thy branches and lordly streams,
Clad in thy blossoming trees,
Mother, giver of ease,
Laughing low and sweet!
Mother, I kiss thy feet,
Speaker soft and low!
Mother, to thee I bow.

[3]
Who hath said thou art weak in thy lands,
When the swords flash out in crores and crores of handsAnd crores and crores of voices roar
Thy dreaded name from shore to shore?
With many strengths who art mighty and stored,
To thee I call, Mother and Lord!
Thou who savest, arise and save!
To her I cry whoever her foemen drove
Back from plain and sea
And shook herself free.

[4]
Thou art wisdom, thou art law,
Thou our heart, our soul, our breath,
Thou the love divine, the awe
In our hearts that conquers death.
Thine the strength that nerves the arm,

Thine the beauty, thine the charm,
Every image, made divine
In our temples, is but thine.
Thou art Durga, Lady and Queen,
With her hands that strike and her swords of sheen.
[5]
Thou art Lakshmi lotus-throned,
And the muse, a hundred-toned,
Pure and perfect, without peer.
Mother, lend thine ear.
Rich with thy hurrying streams,
Bright with thy orchard gleams,
Dark of hue, O candid-fair,
[6]
In thy soul, with jewelled hair,
And thy glorious smile divine,
Loveliest of all earthly lands,
Showering wealth from well-stored hands!
Mother, mother mine!
Mother Sweet, I bow to thee,
Mother, great and free.

The song Vande Mataram was there for over two decades, but its power was battle tested for the first time in the year 1905. Ironically, the opportunity was provided by the courtesy of the British regime when Curzon, the Viceroy of India, partitioned Bengal into two parts, East Bengal for Muslims and West Bengal for Hindus. On paper the plan seemed a very shrewd move and the first cousin of the divide and rule policy. However, when the plan was implemented, almost all the sections of Bengal opposed it, and instead of dividing, it united the people of Bengal. They all, as one body, strongly protested by marching to the tune of Vande Mataram. Such was the magic of Vande Mataram that ordinary people, who so far had never uttered a word against the British regime, openly opposed it.

At that time Gandhiji was testing and perfecting his weapon of Satyagraha in South Africa. He heard about the song and almost instantly developed an affinity for Vande Mataram. In the issue of *The Indian Opinion* dated December 2, 1905, he wrote "every western nation has its national anthem to be sung on important occasions. The song Vande Mataram composed by him (Bankim Chandra) has become so popular throughout India that it has come out to be our national anthem"[78]

A decade later he came to India, joined the Congress, and slowly but surely started transforming it into a real nationalist party. To begin with he started writing his letters with the words 'Vande Mataram' from Mohandas.

Millions of ordinary people pronounced the powerful 'Mantra' of Vande Mataram and became heroes, and thousands chanted it and gallantly kissed the gallows. Notable among them were:

Bhagat Singh—dedicated his life to the liberation of his motherland India. During a meeting of the Central Legislative Assembly in 1929, he along with Batukeshwar Dutt on 8th April hurled a bomb onto the assembly floor and scattered leaflets demanding independence for India. After the explosion of the bomb he did not run away, but at the top of his voice shouted the magic words, Vande Mataram. Hanged by the British regime in March 1931, his last words were, Vande Mataram.

Chandra Shekhar Azad—He was a fearless freedom fighter and a member of the Indian Revolutionary Party. When surrounded by police of the British regime, he refused to surrender, and with revolvers in both hands fought gallantly to the last but one bullet. The last bullet was for himself, and his last word Vande Mataram was for the independence of India.

Jitendranath Mukerjee—He protested against the injustice and brutality of the British regime. When arrested, he drew spiritual strength from the song, Vande Mataram and starved himself to death.

Ashfaqullah Khan—He was a gallant freedom fighter, who by force took away the British government's money chest from the Kakori Mail train to finance the fight against the foreign rule. This 27-year-young revolutionary was caught and hanged at Lyallpur Jail in the year 1927. His last words at the gallows were, Vande Mataram.

Kudiram Bose—He, at the age of fourteen, left school and became a member of the 'Revolutionary Party'. To expose the black deeds of the British regime he printed a pamphlet, the title of which was *Bande Mataram*. To drive out the English, he threw several bombs, including the one at the Bengal Governor's special train. Caught and sentenced to death, this 19-year-old freedom fighter chanted Vande Mataram all the way to the gallows.

Sohan Lal Pathak—He was the joint editor of the magazine *Bande Mataram*. In 1914, he went to California, U.S.A. and joined the 'Gadar Party', which assigned to him the task of motivating the Indian soldiers, stationed at Singapore and Burma, to revolt against the English. The Army at Singapore did revolt in 1915. But when he made a similar attempt in Burma, he was caught and sentenced to death. His last words were Vande Mataram.

Surya Sen and Preeti Lata Waddedar of Bengal—They sacrificed their lives demanding freedom with their courage augmented by the song Vande Mataram.

Subramania Bharti—This great poet of the south, wrote many poems full of patriotism. Vande Mataram found a prominent place of importance in many of his poems. One of his poems was—

Let us chant Vande Mataram
Let us pray to mother India
(English Translation)

The poems inspired many and made them desire independence. One of them was V.O. Chidambaram Pillai, popularly called V. O. C. Pillai.

V.O.C Pillai—He in 1907 started 'The Swadeshi Steam Navigation Company' and challenged the monopoly of the English, over the lucrative maritime trade. Unfair and unjust restrictions were imposed on the Swadeshi Company, but by now V.O.C Pillai had spread the message of Vande Mataram among his workers, and they willingly endured the hardships. The British regime then charged him of sedition on cooked up charges, and to ensure the closure of his navigation company, he was sentenced to the jail, at Andaman Island.

V.O.C Pillai reacted to the injustice by shouts of Vande Mataram, and soon thousands took to the streets in protest; they were wearing badges with Vande Mataram written on them and were chanting Vande Mataram. The British administration came down with a heavy hand on any group found raising the slogan 'Vande Mataram', and brutal force of police *lathis* and bayonets was used to break the spell of Vande Mataram. Many were arrested and beaten up in public for raising the slogan of Vande Mataram.

Bharat Mata Samiti, a group of youngsters was at that time very active and the main aim of that group was to spread patriotism and to preserve the pride of the nation. The Samiti decided that by sentencing V.O.C Pillai, and brutally beating up people for chanting Vande Mataram, an unpardonable act was committed. The Samiti found the district collector Ash responsible for all the atrocities, and unanimously decided to eliminate him.

Vanchi Iyer, a dedicated member of the Bharat Mata Samiti was given the responsibility for the implementation of the decision. A few days later Vanchi confronted the culprit, district collector Ash, at Mahiachi railway station and shot him dead. It was impossible to run away from the crowded railway station, so Vanchi quickly placed the pistol on his temple, shouted the inspiring Vande Mataram three times and pressed the trigger to kill himself. Thus one more gallant son of Bharat Mata had sacrificed his life, whose aim was freedom and Vande Mataram the inspiration.

The list is long for it has thousands of names. The Government of free India brought out an official 'who's who of Indian Martyrs', which has a list of 10000 names of those who were hanged or killed during the freedom struggle. Even this long list was incomplete, as many died anonymously. Without hesitation it can be presumed that each one of them was influenced, in one way or the other, by Vande Mataram.

From the very beginning, India's struggle for freedom was inseparable from Vande Mataram, as it was impossible to plan the independence of India, without first thinking of Vande Mataram. Even those who designed the early Indian national flags could not do so without Vande Mataram.

One of the very first national flags that went up on the Indian soil was on August 7, 1906, at Parsee Bagan in Calcutta, which now is known as the Green Park of Kolkata. It had three strips and the middle yellow strip of this tricolour flag had Vande Mataram written on it in bold deep blue Devanagri script. In the month of December of the same year the Indian National Congress was to meet at Calcutta. Sister Nivedita specially designed a flag for the occasion, which was saffron in colour with the symbol of Vajrast—the weapon of Indra Devta—in the centre and Vande Mataram inscribed just below it. The flag was carried by the students of the school she ran and prominently displayed in the pavilion of the Congress meet.

The influence of Vande Mataram was not confined to the boundaries of India alone, but was also present in distant places. In 1905, Madame Cama attended an international conference at Paris along with a group of freedom fighters from India. There she was required to hoist an Indian flag, and like the previous flags; it too was tricolour but differed in details. This flag also had Vande Mataram written over the middle yellow strip. Madame Came unfurled the flag before the international gathering and declared "This flag is of Indian independence. Behold, it is born..."

In the United States of America, Lala Har Dayal was instrumental in spreading the magic of Vande Mataram, and its impact was instantaneous. There the Indians started greeting each other with the words, Vande Mataram. Bipin Chandra Pal published a magazine *Vande Mataram* so did Lala Lajpat Rai, who brought out a journal *Bande Mataram.* Whenever the aim was freedom, the name was Vande Mataram, and no patriotic Indian could save himself from its influence. If the history of India's struggle for freedom could be condensed to just two words, they would always be Vande Mataram. Before independence, Vande Mataram was the de facto national anthem of India. The *Cambridge History of India* says: "The greatest and most enduring gift of the Swadeshi Movement was Vande Mataram, the uncrowned national anthem (of India)".[79] Poet Rabindranath, in the Congress session of 1896 at Calcutta, was asked to sing not one of his own poems, but Vande Mataram.[80] Once again, when he was returning to India from London, his English friends asked him to sing not one of his own poems, but the song Vande Mataram.[81]

The leaders of India were equivocal at one time or the other, in declaring Vande Mataram as the national anthem of India, Notable among them were:

Maharishi Aurobindo— Vande Mataram was an expression of nationalism, its very soul and therefore the national anthem. It quickly spread throughout India and was on the lips of millions as the national anthem[82]

B.N. Pande—Bankim Chandra Chatterji's poem Vande Mataram first appeared in his novel in 1882 and soon became the Marseillaise of the nationalist movement throughout India.[83]

Jawaharlal Nehru—Vande Mataram, a song which occurs in Bankim Chatterji's novel. The song was quite popular during the nationalist agitation in the early part of this century in Bengal. Subsequently it became a kind of unofficial national anthem.[83]

Balgangadhar Tilak—Vande Mataram, which at the beginning of the 20th century became the anthem of the Indian nationalist movement, is the motherland personified[85]

Rabindranath Tagore—Vande Mataram! These are the magic words which will open the door of his iron safe, break through the walls of his strong room, and confound the hearts of those who are disloyal to its call and to say Vande Mataram.[86]

Mahatma Gandhi—The song Vande Mataram composed by him (Bankim Chandra) has became very popular... The song has proved so popular that it has come to be our national anthem.[87]

When the time came for India to become independent, the whole nation had taken it for granted that Vande Mataram and Vande Mataram alone would be the national anthem of free India, but to the dismay of the hundreds of million, a slave song was selected for that honour, even though the people were against it. In an opinion poll conducted in 1948, by a widely circulated newspaper to find the most acceptable song as the national anthem, an overwhelming majority of about 80 per cent selected Vande Mataram.

The enemies of Vande Mataram were active for over four decades, and they were trying hard to dislodge the song from the affectionate place it had found in the hearts of Indians. But, how could a beautiful song like Vande Mataram have enemies? The cause of enmity was nothing else but the popularity of the song, because this immensely popular song became so intimately associated with the want for freedom that the British regime started to fear it.

Vande Mataram was first published in the year 1882. It had been there for about a quarter of a century, openly sung in largely attended public gatherings, but no objection had ever been raised against it. It was only after the spontaneous and popular opposition of the masses against the partition of Bengal in 1905, and the devastatingly effective use of Vande Mataram, the intrinsic power of the song became apparent to the British regime. Only then did they begin to recognise the song as their enemy. The song had become a threat to their Raj of India, so the might of the British Empire was used to discredit and, if possible, destroy it. In a well-planned strategy, a multi-pronged attack was mounted against Vande Mataram, and it was banned in all the government and government-aided schools. Through a government circular, its officials were prohibited to take part in any meet or function where Vande Mataram was to be sung. Government friendly songs were encouraged and patronised. One such song was Jana Gana Mana, which was frequently recited in many government recognised schools. All were advised to keep away from Vande Mataram, and those who dared to openly sing the song, were flogged and even put behind bars. But the Empire was never able to extinguish the fire that was Vande Mataram. Long before India became free, Vande Mataram was the national anthem of the people.

17

Unmaking of Vande Mataram

The Empire Strikes Back

The British Empire minutely examined the book *Anand Math* and the song Vande Mataram. Under the directions of the Empire, a biased critique was prepared and in this appraisal, both the book and the song were shown as Hindu communal creations. As a result Christians banned the song in their teaching institutions, and many Muslims openly opposed Vande Mataram. It is a well-documented fact that many Muslims gave their liberty and life with Vande Mataram on their lips, but after the Empire sponsored campaigns against the song; many believed that Vande Mataram was a Hindu attack on Islam, and it was their religious duty to oppose the song.

Immediately after the 1905 partition of Bengal by Curzon, a massive political wave of nationalism had followed, and the effect of this wave was not confined to Bengal alone, but was felt all over India. The stories of the 1857 war of independence were still fresh in the memory of the English, and the terrified Westminster called George Nathaniel Curzon back to England in 1905; immediately after the popular protest of the partition of Bengal. Officially, the

Viceroy had resigned over some differences with the Commander-in-Chief of the Indian army Lord Kitchener, but actually it was a polite way to sack Curzon.

The next Viceroy, Lord Minto, was an army man of many years and had fought wars in Afghanistan and Egypt. This battletested man was sent by England to control the political damage caused by the partition of Bengal, and to tame the wave of nationalism that followed it.

Minto's first move was to create an All India Mohammedans Deputation, which called on the Viceroy, for the first time, at Simla on October 1, 1906. The leader of the deputation was His Highness Aga Khan of Bombay, who was one of the many puppets the Empire had in India, to use whenever there was a need. To this man the undeserved status of the 'Leader of the Muslims in India'[88] was bestowed by the Viceroy. This leader of Muslims, at the end of the British Raj, left India abandoning all the Muslims, to live a life of unimaginable luxury and opulence in foreign countries. The Muslim deputation pleaded for 'separate electorates for the Muslims' as they were averse to place their 'national interests at the mercy of an unsympathetic majority' [88], and Lord Minto's response was pregnant with wicked mischief. He said: "I am grateful to you for the opportunity you are affording me of expressing my appreciation of the just aim of the followers of Islam and their determination to share in the political history of our (British) Empire".[88] The draft of Minto's response was carefully worded, and much thought and time was spent to give it the final shape. The Viceroy addressed the Muslims as "the descendants of a conquering and ruling race"[89], with full knowledge that he was letting out a genie of hatred which would embitter the relations between the Hindus and the Muslims for a long time to come, but this was what he wanted.

Under Lord Minto, there was a definite shift in the thinking of the regime. According to Nehru, "British policy became definitely pro-Muslim, or rather in favour of those elements among the Muslims who were opposed to the national movement. But early in the twentieth century the tendency towards nationalism and political activity became more noticeable among the younger generation of Muslims. To divert this and provide a safe channel for it, the Muslim League was started in 1906 under the inspiration of the British government and the leadership of one of its chief supporters, the Aga Khan.[90] Muslims correctly sensed that the British government was seeking their help to weaken the nationalist movement, which was mainly under the control of the Hindus. They also calculated that their help would result in rewards for them. Under Minto, the number of Muslims in the government services rose and at the end of the Raj it was up to sixty per cent at many places.

The poisonous seed sown by Minto, in due course germinated. Constantly nourished by water of hatred, the seedling ultimately grew into a tall poisonous tree, and bore many bitter fruits. One such fruit was Shahid Suhrawardy, and another was Mohammed Ali Jinnah, who promised a blood bath, and during the infamous direct action, the blood of 20,000 Indians—5000 killed and 15,000 wounded— was flowing over the streets of Calcutta.

The second session of the 'All India Muslim League' was held at Amritsar on December 30, 1908, whose elected president for the year was Syed Ali Imam. He said in his presidential address:

"I cannot say what you think, but when I find the most advanced province (Bengal) of India put forward the sectarian cry of Vande Mataram as national cry and the sectarian Rakhi-Bandhan as national observance, my heart is filled with despair and disappointment, and the suspicion that under the clock of nationalism Hindu nationalism is preached in India, becomes a conviction. I ask the architects of Indian nationalism, both in Calcutta and Poona; do they expect the Mossalmans of India to accept Vande Mataram and Sivaji celebrations? The Mohammedans may be weak in any thing you please, but they are not weak in cherishing the traditions of their glorious past."

Syed Ali Imam forgot, as do most Muslim leaders of the day, that the overwhelming majority of India's Muslims are converted Hindus and not the descendants of Turks, Pathans or Mughals, and their glorious past was nothing but Hindu history. Noted writer Durga Das says: "Today those who can trace their ancestry to these conquering races are only a drop in the ocean of Indian humanity".[91] Both Mohammad Iqbal, who conceptualised Pakistan, and Mohammad Ali Jinnah, who demanded Pakistan, had a Hindu past. The great grandfather of Iqbal was a *Sapru gotra* Kashmiri Brahmin, and only a few generations back the ancestors of Jinnah were Hindus.

Efforts made by Lord Minto and the British regime to discredit Vande Mataram were slowly showing results, and the first open criticism of Vande Mataram was heard at the meeting of the Muslim League, held in 1907, where some delegates drew attention of the house and complained that Vande Mataram was a Hindu song and all Muslims should boycott it. They were obviously influenced by the propaganda made by the British administration against the novel *Anand Math*, and many believed it without realising the fact that the song was actually written several years before and independently of the novel.[167] As planned by the British regime, Muslims started to oppose Vande Mataram, which was evident at the subsequent meetings of the League, but before long there was the First World War, in which the very survival of the British Empire was at stake. As a result, the whole attention of the government was preoccupied by the war efforts and the aftermaths of the war, and nothing of significance happened with the song Vande Mataram, till 1923.

Pd. Vishnu Digambar Paluskar was a reputed musician of nationwide fame, and was regarded with great respect by the different national leaders associated with independence agitation. Since 1915, Pd. Puluskar used to attend every Congress session, and captivate the delegates by singing Vande Mataram in a melodious tone. The 38th Congress session was held at CoConada in 1923, whose president, Maulana Mohammad Ali, was a 45-year-old Aligarh educated graduate. The specially erected pandal was full with over 6,000 delegates. Jawaharlal Nehru was present on the dais as one of the general secretaries.

When Vishnu Digambar rose to sing Vande Mataram, in conformity with tradition, Maulana Sahib raised an objection on the ground that music was taboo to his religion. The assembled leaders were completely bewildered, but Vishnu Digambar was incensed and hit back: "This is a national forum and not the platform of any single community. This is no mosque to object to music. There is no justification for a ban on music here. When the president could put up with music in the presidential procession, why does he object to it here?" Having silenced the president and without waiting for his reply, he proceeded to sing Vande Mataram and completed it. Respect for his sense of national pride and love for the motherland grew. The people admired his moral courage and applauded him heartily.[92]

All over India people were shocked by the opposition to their much loved song by the Congress president on the flimsy ground that it was against the Muslim sentiments. In fact, it all was a part of an ingenious plan of the British government in cahoots with the Muslim League. According to the plan, the song Vande Mataram was to be communalised by canards, and made controversial to such an extent that Hindus could never hope to project it as an acceptable song of the nation. With this aim, the League further increased opposition to Vande Mataram and took the stand that "Singing of Vande Mataram is a declaration of war on Islam".

It always was a prominent policy of the Congress to appease Muslims, and once again, to satisfy and calm their hurt feelings, a meeting of the Congress working committee was convened in October 1937 at Calcutta, under the chairmanship of Jawaharlal Nehru. The working committee deliberated for long over the issue and adopted a lengthy statement on Oct. 28, 1937. The statement read:

"The committee recognises the validity of the objections raised by Muslim friends (Those who were rabidly critical of Vande Mataram were officially declared by Congress as friends) to certain parts of the song. While the committee has taken note of such objection insofar as it has intrinsic value, the committee wishes to point out that the modern evolution of the use of the song as part of national life is of infinitely greater importance than its setting in a historical novel before the national movement had taken shape. Taking all things into consideration, therefore, the committee recommends that wherever Vande Mataram is sung at national gatherings, only the first two stanzas should be sung, with perfect freedom to the organisations to sing any other song of an unobjectionable character, in addition to , or in place of Vande Mataram song." In this Congress statement, the provision of "... any other song" and "in place of Vande Mataram" was to particularly hurt the song. The injuries it caused were grave.

Strangely, the committee failed to take note of three important facts:

(i) The Muslim leaders who objected to the song Vande Mataram never opposed it during the Khilafat Movement organised by the Congress, along with the various Muslim organisations, on the dismemberment of Turkey, after her defeat in the First World War. At that time, all the Muslims used to sing Vande Mataram without any hesitation.[170]

(ii) The 'Foemen' of the song could never be the Muslims. When the 'seventy million voices' of the original song roared, it obviously included all the Muslims as well, because at that time the total population of Bengal province was seventy million.

(iii) Vande Mataram was written almost five years earlier than the novel, *Anand Math.* In the literary circles of Bengal its independent existence was a well recognised fact.[171]

But the League was after the blood of Vande Mataram, and so even this Congress appeasement failed to satisfy the Muslims. The Muslim League, which was determined to destroy the religious harmony of India, intensified its opposition to Vande Mataram, and Jinnah now demanded the death of Vande Mataram and declared: "The Muslims would never accept the song"[93], as a result in legislative assemblies, the Muslim League members started boycotting the singing of Vande Mataram, and raised point of order or even staged walk-outs to avoid the singing of Vande Mataram. The Congress had already accepted to sing only the first two non-controversial stanzas of the song, and to further calm the Muslims the practice to recite from the holy Koran was started from January 1938. But these steps failed to mollify the Muslims, and the League, whose undeclared policy was to hurt the Hindu sentiments, adamantly demanded the very deletion of Vande Mataram from the national movement for independence. The Congress was mischievously regarded as a Hindu organisation by the Muslim League, which was always in search of ways to quarrel with it. The League passed a resolution listing the grievances of Muslims, knowing well that the demands were unreasonable and would never be accepted by the Congress. Vande Mataram was on top of that list.

By 1946, it was clear that Muslims will never live with Hindus. Firoze Khan Noon and Shahid Suhrawardy—both future Prime Ministers of Pakistan—publicly declared that there would be a blood bath, the like of which India had never seen so far, should Muslims be denied a separate state. True to their words there were communal clashes all over India and under 'Direct Action', in Calcutta alone, in a matter of days, the blood of over 20,000 innocents was flowing on the streets of the city. The official figure was 5000 dead and 15,000 wounded, unofficially 16000 were murdered, and perhaps 40,000 wounded. In Noakhali, 5000 more died in a week.[94] The partition of India was a catastrophic event for the nation, in which about one million died[95] and another 10 million had to leave their homes[96] to become refugees and muhajirs.

After paying such a heavy price for the creation of Pakistan and to satisfy Muslims, all, especially Hindus, believed that each and every Muslim with uncompromising beliefs would now move to the nation of his choice, and leave the Hindus to live the way they liked, without any further interference. Even if Jains, Sikhs and Boddhas are not taken into account, as historically they have been intimately related to the Hindu religion, the communities of Parsis, Bohras, Khozas and even Christians have been living for centuries with Hindus, without friction, and the prosperity of the nation was shared with them, with pleasure. Parsis and Bohras continue to be one of the richest in India and Hindus have ever since rejoiced their ever increasing prosperity. The decision of those Muslims, who had decided to stay back in India, was taken as their consent to live with Hindus in brotherhood of love and peace. It was hoped that their opposition to the favourite song of the nation would now cease forever.

When on August 15, 1947, India became an independent nation, everyone was looking forward to the long awaited moment when their beloved song, Vande Mataram, would become the national anthem of India, but strange things happened, and Vande Mataram was not given its due status.

18

Empire Employs Mountbatten

Hired to Divide India

On May 5, 1945, Germany surrendered and after five years and eight months of war, the guns in Europe stopped spitting fire, but it was only the end of the European part of the Second World War. Japan it came to a stop, three months nine days and two Atom Bombs later, where on August 10, 1945 the guns finally went silent, after her unconditional surrender.

Long overdue, because of the Second World War, British general elections were held in July 1945. Winston Churchill was the undisputed leader and much admired Prime Minister of Britain. During the war, under his leadership, Britain had faced many reverses and setbacks, but at the end a victorious Britain had emerged. This triumph had made Churchill, and his Conservative Party, to dream of a comfortable victory in the elections. However people had not forgotten his promise to offer nothing else but "Blood, toil, tears and sweat". From the beginning of the war, year after year, Britain was starving and shivering in the freezing cold, and lucky were those, who could have a hot water bath, for in most of the households hot water, even for a pot of tea, was not available on all days. Although Britain had emerged victorious in the war, but this victory had almost vanquished her. Only six years ago every citizen of this small island nation of 50 million was the proud owner of a powerful and prosperous empire, but by the election time the arrogance was taken over by the misery. With crippled industries and bankrupt treasury, there was an unbearably severe rationing of each consumer product. What to talk about food, fuel and fabrics, even sugar, soap and shoelaces were not available. The starving Britons had taken their decision, if this was the price for the empire they were not interested, and the only thing the voters now wanted, was a full stomach. The desire of the people for a peaceful future was the cause of the humiliating defeat of the Conservatives, and Churchill, instead of Prime Minister became the leader of the opposition. The overwhelming majority of the thirty million British voters cast their votes in favour of the Labour Party. In a historic landslide victory, Clement Richard Attlee became the Prime Minister of Britain, who had publicly committed to give freedom to the Indians.

Churchill knew well that India was the foundation on which the entire British Empire was standing, and without India the whole Empire would crumble. In the parliament he once said: "The loss of India would be final and fatal to us. It could not fail to be part of a process that would reduce us to the scab of a minor power".[97] He would never have agreed for the dissolution of the Empire. King George VI revealed in his book *His life and Reign* that "Churchill was aware that India could not be held indefinitely", and had decided to eventually "give up India to Indians", but Churchill had wished the eventuality to come only after a dozen decades. To clear any doubt, Churchill had declared: "Let there be no mistake about it in any quarter. We mean to hold on our own. I have not become the King's minister in order to preside over the liquidation of the British Empire".[98] Long ago Rudyard Kipling had said: "The responsibility for governing India has been placed by the inscrutable decree of providence upon the shoulders of the British race" and Churchill believed each word of it.

Both, Attlee and Churchill, loved Britain, and one was as loyal as the other was, but they differed greatly in their approaches. Churchill would have persuaded the people to sacrifice a bit more to keep the Empire intact, while Attlee felt that Britain was no longer in a position to pay the price for her maintenance. By the time the Second World War was about to end, Britain was reduced to the status of a junior partner of the Allied forces, even though the British Empire was still intact and not an inch of her territory was lost. But one thing that Britain had lost was her youth power, the most essential ingredient required for sustaining the life of the Empire. By 1946, there were barely a thousand British ICS officers who, with 30, 000 soldiers of their race, were somehow holding 330 million Indians in their administrative grasp, which every day was becoming more and more loose. The relentless rain of bombs by Stuka and Messerschmitt bombers of Luftwaffe — the German air force — had reduced Britain to rubble and ruined her industries. Whatever manpower was left, was needed for the reconstruction of the nation, and could not be spared for administering the Empire. The British government had to let India go, for it was no longer in a position to hold her.

When the moment came to defeat Hitler, an American sitting in Washington D.C. was the man who gave the final order. That man was Franklin Delano Roosevelt, and he happened to be the President of the United States of America. Churchill was against the 1944 invasion of France, but he was overruled by Roosevelt. When the Allied Forces started landing on the Normandy beach on D-Day, they were under the command of Dwight D. Eisenhower who too was an American, and as the Supreme Allied Commander of all the combined force was giving orders to the British Generals. London was no longer the hub of power, and the days of glory were over for the British Empire. In India, after three and a half event-packed centuries, the eternal time wheel was about to complete its turn and it was not in the power of any human being to stop it.

It was sheer good luck for India that Attlee became the Prime Minister of Britain, who, unlike Churchill, could clearly see the turning time-wheel, and soon after assuming power, decided to free India. Lord Wavell was the Viceroy of India, and his open pro-Muslim posture had permanently antagonised the Congress. All his moves were bogged down in the quagmire of political mistrust and communal hatred. Obviously, a new face with fresh ideas and unorthodox approach was needed at Delhi, for the successful winding up of the Empire, and Attlee handpicked forty-six-year-old Admiral Viscount Mountbatten of Burma, for the job.

Although the appointment of Mountbatten was final by the month of January 1947, the fact was not made public, and even Wavell was not informed of the change. These gave Mountbatten an opportunity to quietly prepare for his new post and decide on his moves, and only when he was ready the Prime Minister on February 20, 1947 announced in parliament the firm intention of Britain to leave India not later than June 1948. He also publicly disclosed that to implement it Lord Mountbatten had been chosen, who would succeed Wavell as Viceroy. Wavell was informed only a few days before the change, which was unusual, for Viceroys were always given six months notice before being sacked. Wavell was given only one.

Mountbatten, through a circuitous way, was the great grandson of Queen Victoria. His friends called him Dicky, and this six feet tall man was so handsome that he "looked like a film star".[99]

When on March 22, Mountbatten rode to the Viceroy's House in a gold gilded landau; Wavell was out on the staircase to receive him. This again was unusual, for in the past outgoing never met the incoming Viceroy to avoid the embarrassment of the sacked Viceroy. Was it done deliberately to enhance the credibility of the new Viceroy?

Perhaps, for Lady Mountbatten was heard by her Indian staff declaring loudly that Vicereine Wavell dressed like her maid servant.[100] Mountbattens were aware that the Indian staff were in the process of discarding old loyalties and acquiring new ones, and such a comment was sure to be disclosed to the soon-to-be new political masters of India. The Mountbattens were highly polished and sophisticated members of the British royal family, and were well aware of the protocol. It was most unusual for them to treat the Wavells in such an offensive way, unless it all was done under a carefully worked out plan to ensure a favourable entry for the Mountbattens into the power circle of the Congress, where Wavell had earned a bad name. Otherwise also the Mountbattens were least interested in maintaining the age-old traditions of the Viceroyalty, for they were the last of the breed. With their departure the species of Viceroys was going to be extinct.

On March 24, 1947 Lord Mountbatten was sworn in as the twentieth Viceroy of India at a glittering ceremony held in the Durbar Hall of his official house. His wife Edwina though always looked charming, but on that day was ravishingly beautiful in the full-length white silk gown she was wearing. The silk was imported from China, and the gown was especially hand-stitched for the occasion. There was a single strand pearl necklace round her slender neck, which was a present from her husband, who bought it from Cairo for the size and lustre of the pearls. To enhance her beauty, a glittering tiara was sitting on her silky brown hair. The tiara, a family gift, was masterly crafted in 1910 by the famous Cartier of Paris, and was made of circular cut brilliant white diamonds set in solid platinum. It was meant to be worn on special occasions like this. Edwina, wrapped in clinging silk with a glittering tiara in her hair and a bewitching smile on her lips, was the most glamorous beauty present under the circular dome of the Durbar Hall. If beauty alone could ever kill, she on that day amply qualified and the first casualty was a man sitting in the first row. His name was Jawaharlal Nehru and he was soon going to be the Prime Minister of India. He, during a trip to Singapore, had already met the Mountbattens but that was a casual meet. On that occasion he had failed to appreciate the charm of the war-weary Edwina, but this time he was thoroughly dazzled by her beauty.

During the years spent at Harrow and Trinity, the prominent education centres of England, Nehru had developed an affinity for things which were English. According to Durga Das "he was an Englishman in Indian skin".[101] Britain had also discovered the qualities of an Englishman in him. It was in their interest to have an Indian Englishman as the first Prime Minister of free India, so they started to build his reputation. When Nehru went to Singapore in March 1946, to inaugurate an Indian war memorial, The Mountbattens were there as it was the SEAC Head quarters. Only recently Nehru had come out from a British jail, yet he was received by the British Commander-in-Chief with such warmth, as is generally reserved for a visiting national dignitary. He was given a red carpet reception and Mountbatten even rode in an open car through the main streets of Singapore, with Nehru by his side. Staff members of SEAC, unaware of the shift in the British policy, pointed to Mountbatten that he was dignifying an anti-British who till recently was a prisoner in their jail. His reply was "Dignify him? It is he who has dignified me, one day this man will be Prime Minister of India".[102] This remark was prominently quoted by the Indian press, which was still under the governing powers of Britain. The exercise to influence the selection of the first Indian Prime Minister had started. Viceroy Wavell had announced on August 12, 1946 that he was going to invite the Congress president to form a provisional government, and on 2nd September Nehru was sworn in as the interim Prime Minister. Five months before anyone in India could even guess, thousands of kilometres away in Singapore, Mountbatten knew that Nehru— whom he was meeting for the first time—was going to be the Prime Minister of India.

India was to be given independence and the first step was the formation of a provisional government, headed by an Indian. At this juncture the post of the Congress president assumed great importance as Wavell was expected to invite him to form the interim government. Most of the Provincial Congress Committees (PCC) had recommended the name of Sardar Patel and a few for Rajendra Prasad, and none had suggested the name of Jawaharlal, but Gandhi wanted Nehru, and respecting his wishes, the name of Jawaharlal was proposed and accepted. At the insistence of Gandhi the down-to-earth organiser (Sardar Patel) was rejected and a high-flown idealist was accepted.[103] The glamour of Nehru made Gandhi bypass his trusted and tested lieutenant Patel, who was with the masses and an Indian inside out. When the Mahatma was questioned about his choice, he replied "Jawahar is the only Englishman in my camp...He is better known abroad than Sardar and will make India play a (greater) role in international affairs."[104] Nehru did shine internationally with his policies of non-alignment, Panchsheel and Hindi Chini Bhai Bhai. However these policies proved to be futile when the Chini Bhai stabbed the Hindi Bhai, in the back.

Mountbatten

Before the year 1946 could end, Attlee, the British Prime Minister, had decided to change the Indian Viceroy, and Mountbatten was his hand-picked choice. When the job was first offered to Mountbatten, he hesitated and was reluctant to accept the responsibility, but after consulting his friends and advisers, he agreed. He knew that the task before him was onerous and complex.

His father, Admiral Louis Alexander Battenberg, had left Germany and his German parents at the age of fourteen, to join the Royal Navy of Britain, and eventually became the First Sea Lord of the Royal Navy. Because of intense anti-German sentiments, during the First World War, his father was forced to resign, and as a precaution for the future the family name was changed from Battenberg to Mountbatten.

During his days in the navy and as the Supreme Commander of South East Asia, Admiral Mountbatten had learnt the value of meticulous planning. He asked for three months time to prepare, which was reluctantly granted. Actually he took two months and twenty days, and during this period, Mountbatten met everyone of importance and anyone capable of giving any useful information on India. He also met his cousin, King George VI, and the war time Prime Minister Winston Churchill, who was now the leader of the opposition. In the end he had many meetings with the Prime Minister, Clement Attlee.

The meeting with George was brief; actually it was a courtesy call by a Viceroy, who was supposed to the representative the King George, who somehow could not gain as much popularity during the just concluded war, as his father could during the World War of his time. One of the reasons was that the battle ground of the first war was the mainland Europe, and the island of Britain had remained unscathed. But during the second war, the Luftwaffe had ruined vast areas of England. As a result, by the end of the war the life of an ordinary Briton had become unbearable and miserable. Another reason was that the much loved King Edward was still alive. Because of his sudden and unexpected abdication the second choice George became the occupant of the British throne, for which he was neither trained nor prepared. It was not that George was not aware of the reality, but he still did very little to enhance the sagging popularity of the royal family.

King George VI

During the wartime bombing, when a part of Buckingham Palace was damaged, his press attaché had tried to win back the sympathies of the public by releasing photographs, in which the King was shown with small firearms, and issuing a sentimental royal declaration to defend the nation. These efforts might have added to his popularity, but were miserably inadequate and failed to restore the prestige of the royal family, which it had during the regime of his father, King George V.

His father was the only British King, who had visited India. Though that was almost 35 years ago, yet he still vividly remembered the stories his father had told him about India. He had told him about the first glimpse he had of India form the deck of his royal ship. He was miles away, but he could see the massive yellow stone arch, the Gateway of India, erected specially in honour of his visit. When one of his ADCs had pointed out the engraving on the summit of the arch, he was so far away that he could not read a word of it, but the captain of the ship immediately arranged for a telescope, and each word became clear to him. He was now able to read 'Erected to commemorate the landing in India of their imperial Majesties, George V and Queen Mary on the second December MCMXI'. The words of Rudyard Kipling: "The responsibility of governing India had been placed by the inscrutable decree of providence upon the shoulders of the British race" came rushing back to his memory. He had always believed in each word written by the first British Nobel laureate of Literature, and the sight of the Gateway of India only reaffirmed his faith, in his race.

His father had also told him about the magnificent Delhi Durbar, where he was coronated, about the fascinating Indian rajas present there in their glittering best, about the colourfully decorated elephants and horses. Once he had told him, about the loyalty of the Indians and the madness with which they showed it off; about his visit to Calcutta, the capital of India; about the Bengalis who lived there, and were his most loyal subjects; about a poem which was very cleverly crafted to praise him, and in the poem the way India—a nation of 300 million—was made to prostate at his feet and beg for mercy, moved him like no other poem could.

His father had told him about the fascinating hunting parties where it was usual to shoot up to ten tigers a day, and once "he claimed twenty-four of the thirty-nine tigers killed". [105] At that time George was a young lad of seventeen and did not believe his father's hunting stories and doubts lingered till he himself was a king, and his very first Viceroy to India—Lord Linlithgow (1936-44)—was officially recorded to have killed 120 tigers, 27 leopards and 38 rhinos during his tenure in India. When one naturalist asked the Viceroy the reason for killing so many tigers, his reply was: "These were Indian tigers, were they not?" Had the British rule lasted for another 25 years, the English would have killed even the last tiger in India.

When his father narrated the Indian stories to him, the glory of the British Empire was at its zenith. But thirty-three years and two World Wars later, when Mountbatten made the courtesy call, gloom had filled the Empire. George was aware that his cousin would shortly be going to India to start the liquidation of the British Empire, but was unaware of the presence of a few killer cells, slowly multiplying deep inside him, which one day were to overwhelm his body. He died of lung cancer on February 6, 1952. On that day he was also unaware that the twenty-one-year old lady sitting at a distance from him in another room would one day ascend the throne of Britain, only to lose the Empire, piece by piece. When in Hong Kong, on June 30, 1997, the Union Jack was hauled down for the last time; it marked the end of a dream which was the British Empire. The Empire where the sun never set was reduced to an island territory, where the sun was seen for a few hours, that too, only on days when the weather remained kind.

Had George known all this, he would have also remembered the name of the British Queen who gave the charter to the East India Company was Elizabeth, the first ever queen of England to have this name. She had put her seal on a document that laid the foundation of the Empire. For the next three hundred and fifty years, no one with the same name would sit on the British throne. He himself was the 6th George and the King before him was the 8th Edward, but Elizabeth remained only one. Time was waiting for the second Elizabeth to ascend the throne, for the one with the name of only Elizabeth was to seal the document, which was to be the end of the Empire.

The glory of the Empire was still intact in the psyche of George, who wished for the success of Mountbatten, and asked him to preserve the dignity of the Crown. He wanted to say a few more words, but suddenly started stammering. Shy, young George was raised under the strict discipline of his German mother and used to stammer, a habit which made him even shyer. Speech therapy and professional guidance from experts had almost cured him, and he was now able to speak fluently, but still stammered on rare occasions, especially when he was tense. Mountbatten knew it, and when George started stammering he sat still, without any expression on his face, waiting for the tension subside. George remembering the instructions of his speech therapist, stopped speaking and took a few slow and deep breaths to ease him, and was soon normal again and resumed the dialogue, this time speaking slowly and articulating each word carefully. George was about to make a sentimental request.

Slowly and carefully George bared his thoughts before Mountbatten. He told him about the stories he had heard, and the attachment his father had to the British monuments in India, especially the life size statue of himself near the India Gate of New Delhi. He also told the Viceroy about his fears, for he believed that the memorials, statues and many other symbols of the British Raj might offend the free nation and could be demolished, once India was left to the Indians. He asked, which sounded almost like a request, Mountbatten to use his charm and power to ensure the safety of the British monuments, and forge some sort of permanent link with India, like joining the British Commonwealth.

The King's appeal and Mountbatten's efforts were effective. India joined the British Commonwealth, and after the English left, not a single statue of a king or any of his knights was pulled down. Half a century after independence, the Gateway of India is still announcing the 'landing in India of their Imperial Majesties' in the land of Shivaji, and in Jana Gana Mana, one thousand million Indians are still singing the praise of a British King.

Winston Churchill

The post of the Indian Viceroy was filled according to the choice of the British Prime Minister and the King formally approved it by affixing his seal. Winston Churchill, the leader of the opposition, had no role to play in the selection. Yet, Attlee insisted on Mountbatten meeting Churchill. There was a valid reason behind it, for the Conservative Party of Churchill was in a clear majority in the House of Lords, and if Churchill desired, any bill for the independence of India could be effectively blocked at Lords, the upper house of Britain, for one or even two years. Attlee was not at all prepared for such a long delay.

Churchill knew Mountbatten well, whose father had served under him in the navy while he was the First Sea Lord, and had given Mountbatten his first major war command, leading to a relationship in which both had a clear understanding of each other.

When Mountbatten came to meet Churchill, he was not in the best of moods as there were many things to upset him. As if the humiliation of defeat in the elections was not enough, the Labour Party, regarded by him as a bunch of half-witted unpatriotic idiots, had decided to let India go free, even though he had warned repeatedly that the loss of India would be fatal to the Empire. India, the most glittering jewel of the Empire, where he had spent many years of his youth playing polo, hunting tigers, sticking pigs and fighting as a British soldier, was loved by Churchill in a special way. India was his blind spot, but he knew India only as well as King George III knew America. Both were totally ignorant of the ground realities.

When on February 20, 1947 the British Prime Minister Attlee announced: "His Majesty's government wishes to make it clear, that it is their definite intention to take the necessary steps to effect the transference of power in to responsible Indian hands by a date not later than June 1948", out of all the members present on that day in the House of Commons, Churchill was hurt most. Along with his statement, Attlee had presented a long list of figures which showed why after the war it was not possible for Britain to rule India. Churchill tried in vain to reverse the flow of the tide by pleading in the House: "This whole business was an attempt by the government to make use of brilliant war figures in order to cover up a melancholy of a disastrous transaction". He was visibly sentimental, when he said: "It is with deep grief that I watch the clattering down of the British Empire with all its glories and all the services it had rendered to mankind. Many have defended Britain against her foes. None can defend her against herself. Let us not hurry, let us not add by shameful flight, by a premature, hurried scuttle". The oration was brilliant and even touching, but it could not delay the setting of the sun. By a convincing majority, the Commons voted for the end of British rule in India.

Only a few days earlier the Commons had rejected Churchill's proposal, and on the day Mountbatten visited him, he was uncomfortable by the cold brought by the freezing gale coming from the direction of the north. There was nothing to warm the fireplace and the whole house was ice cold. With experience, Churchill had found that the warmest place of his house was his own bed, where he could keep himself warm and safe under the thick layer of a feather-filled quilt. It seemed that Clementine Hozier, Churchill's wife, was expecting Mountbatten, for she came dressed to greet the guest. Freshly baked cookies and tea with real milk soon followed, which in those days were luxuries that were not found in every house of London. Churchill after all was the leader of the opposition with the rank of a cabinet minister, and the post had certain privileges attached to it. While Mountbatten was munching cookies, a few British officers in India were packing their baggage for the final journey back to their homes in England. Their Indian staff observed: "you have been living in a land of milk and honey, now you are going to a land in debt to the world, where everything is rationed except air".[106]

Both tea and pleasantries were soon over and now it was time for the real talk, where one was a master craftsman and the other a plain novice in the art of real politics, and each knew the strengths as well as weaknesses of the other. Mountbatten was tense because Churchill's answer was crucial for his success in India, though he was prepared to hear the same 'no' that Churchill for the last 40 years was handing out to everyone, who arrived with the proposal to dismantle his beloved Empire. Once, even Franklin D. Roosevelt was given a firm' no' by Churchill, when during a meeting in 1941 over the 'Atlantic Charter' the independence of India was mentioned in their discussions. Churchill, along with other Allies, was prepared to be kind to all the nations of the world after the war was over, but India was to be excluded from the generous provisions of the charter. At subsequent meetings also, Churchill was often remembered for his famous remark: "I have not become His Majesty's First Minister to preside over the dissolution of the British Empire".

Mountbatten knew, if he wanted that elusive 'yes' from Churchill, he would have to agree to certain demands, and with this in mind, he hesitatingly presented his case. Churchill already knew all the figures and was aware of the facts which made it impossible for Britain to rule India any longer. The cost, both in manpower and money, was enormous and beyond the means of Britain, but he was against any shameful flight.

Churchill disclosed to Mountbatten about a meeting he had with Jinnah, when he was on a visit to London and had quietly come to meet and beg his help in the creation of Pakistan, a separate nation for the Muslims of India. He had assured him that the new Muslim nation would always be prepared to cooperate and safeguard the British interests in Asia. Jinnah had also reminded him that during the just concluded war, the Muslim League had actively supported the British regime, while on the other hand the Hindu dominated Congress, instead of helping had started the 'Quit India' agitation, and had placed the British government in a difficult position. In the future also, Britain could never expect any worthwhile support from the Hindu-dominated India. The division of India appealed to Churchill, for he had never relished the idea of an independent nation, ten times the size of Britain, coming into existence, that one day could challenge her power. He insisted upon Mountbatten that India must be divided before letting her go free, only then the Conservatives might think over it and extend their support to the legislation for the independence of India.

In the month of December 1946, Wavell accompanied by Nehru, Baldev Singh, Jinnah and Liaquat Ali flew to

London, to work out a compromise for setting up the constituent assembly. There Jinnah showed remarkable determination in wrecking any formula that had the potential of being successful. The visit to London proved to be a futile exercise and Nehru with Baldev Singh returned to India. However Jinnah stayed back and during this stay he lobbied extensively for the creation of Pakistan, and delivered many vicious speeches against Hindus and their leaders. He also had several meetings with Churchill, some openly and the rest under cover. Churchill informed that ever since Jinnah was in constant secret contact with him.[107] He advised Mountbatten to trust Jinnah, for his demand for Pakistan would prove beneficial for Britain. Moreover, unless a separate Muslim nation was created, Jinnah would not let peace prevail in India.[108] He reminded him of the vow taken by Jinnah: "We shall have India divided or we shall have India destroyed." On that day, the novice Mountbatten had learnt a lot about the murky side of politics from the master of the art. He assured Churchill of his unwavering loyalty to the Crown and complete dedication to the interest of the Empire.

Clement Attlee

Clement Attlee became the Prime Minister when Britain was passing through a very critical time. The nation never had to face so many problems, all of which were grave and had come together. Britain was in debt to the world to the extent of 2730 million pounds, mostly to the United States. In addition she even owed India 1300 million pounds, [109] a situation which was unimaginable before the war. It was like a slave giving a loan to his master. The war had made it possible.

On a visit to London, Wavell had explained about two options to Attlee that were available to Britain. One was to continue the Raj of India, for which an additional force of at least one hundred thousand British troops were required.

The other was to leave India at an early date, after which the responsibility of governing India would be passed on to the Indians.[110] If Britain at that time could spare just one lakh (1,00,000) Britons to soldier for the Crown and pay for their salaries, India even today would have been a part of the British Empire. To say the same thing differently, had there been no world wars, Britain would have had enough money and manpower to rule India for several hundred more years. In the two world wars, Britain had lost about one million of her finest fighting men. In the First World War 7,02,000 of them died and in the second their number was 2,33,042.[111]The role of the two wars was decisive in letting India go free, from the yoke of slavery.

Attlee knew that to provide an additional fighting force was impossible for him. The youths of Britain were fed up of military service; moreover the financial resources to maintain such a large force were not available to the bankrupt government of Britain. The only available source of money was America and the sentiments of that country were such that she would never have funded an army to keep India in slavery.

Britain had fought the Second World War under the doctrine of a just fight against the evil of Germany, who wanted to subjugate the whole world, but in India, Britain herself was a subjugator, and by the same doctrine had lost the moral right to rule India. Not only that, America also was of the firm opinion that Britain, after the world war, should grant freedom to India. Before the situation in India could go out of control, Attlee wanted to quit India, but in a fashion that was in the best interest of Britain .The man selected by him for the job was Mountbatten, and to impress upon everyone the urgency of the situation, he committed His Majesty's Government by a declaration in parliament on February 20, 1947, that India would be freed by June 1948. After this public announcement, no less then sixteen months time was available for all those, who were responsible for the transfer of power in India. Mountbatten, who was given the job in January 1947, had one and a half years for the completion of his assignment, and all concerned agreed that this time was enough for it.

A few days before his departure to India, Mountbatten had a number of meetings with Attlee because there were many plans to discuss and several instructions to take. It was the last meeting, and all the issues had been discussed. It was time to conclude it, and Mountbatten was mentally waiting for the hint to go. Had he not been attentive, he certainly would have missed the sudden change in the tone of his boss, who was now speaking in a monotone, as if a giant drone was humming. They were all alone in the sound proof meeting room; still the British Prime Minister lowered his voice, as if he was going to divulge some very important secret. Mountbatten moved a few inches closer to his master, who was now speaking on the changed political scenario of the world, brought about by the war. Attlee explained that many countries, including Germany, France, Italy and Japan, so far regarded as world powers, were reduced to nothing. Even Great Britain in future would not be able to influence the world from the same position of power, which she had enjoyed so far. In a war of this magnitude such changes were expected, but the change which worried him most was the rise of the military might of Stalin. The swiftness, with which the Russian army took control of Poland, Hungary, Czechoslovakia and other Eastern European territories, was really disturbing. Even in Germany the Red army had occupied the biggest chunk of land, and was first to enter Berlin. The British government was of the opinion that the Russians would not rest at their present position, and in future would march into Asia to increase their sphere of influence. In an event like this, Britain would never trust the independent India, ruled by Gandhi's Congress government — who had lost his confidence after the Quit-India movement and non-cooperation in the war efforts of the British government. At this point, Attlee paused for a long time, and then resumed speaking slowly, emphasising each word: "After due consideration, His Majesty's government has reached the conclusion that the creation of Pakistan is essential to safeguard the Western strategic interests" [112]. Though, Attlee warned, the division of India would not be an easy task, because Congress, the main political party of India, was against it, and as long as the party was under the influence of Mr. Gandhi, it would never accept the division. Mountbatten informed his boss that he was aware of the reality, and to deal with it had prepared a plan. He had met Nehru in Singapore and probably knew the way to influence him, and once he was with him, the task would be easy. He assured the Prime Minister that he was a loyal and dedicated servant of His Majesty, and would never spare any effort to complete the task assigned to him.

Mountbatten explained to the Prime Minister that in India he would face a very complex situation, and to effectively deal with it, would require a strong supporting team. He was given as his Chief of Staff General Lord Ismay, who was a very able officer in the Ministry of Defence, where he was Churchill's right hand man, during the period of the war. Ismay came to India along with a team comprising of several supporting hands. Mountbatten knew that his work in India would generate many controversies, so he demanded a press attaché to present his views and himself to India and to the international community in a favourable way. So far none of his nineteen predecessors from Lord Canning to Lord Wavell ever had a press attaché. Alan Campbell Johnson accompanied him to India as his press attaché. He made a request and got an aircraft for his own use. A Lancaster bomber of Second World War vintage was refitted, for his exclusive use, even though the ride in the belly of the bumpy bomber was far from being comfortable, but it was the best that Britain of that day could provide to her Viceroy. Three and a half centuries earlier, when William Hawkins, the first Englishman of the East India Company, sailed in his galleon *Hector*, he took more than six months to reach Delhi from London. Mountbatten, in his Lancaster, covered the same distance in two days.

Mountbatten made his last request, when the meeting was about to be over. He first explained to his boss the need for an efficient intelligence team by quoting many instances of unrest and near mutiny, which occurred recently in several parts of India. Only the previous year — in February and March 1946 — ordinary people had joined the mutiny of sailors of the Royal Indian Navy (RIN), stationed at Bombay, in which about 1500 people had died in the gun battle that followed. Wavell had to face a difficult situation because he had not a single word of warning from the intelligence units. Mountbatten submitted that such a situation may endanger his carefully prepared plans, and pointed out that with the end of the war several units of MI-5, the intelligence wing of the army, were now idle. The highly experienced and resourceful men of these units were the masters of their trade, and for them nothing was impossible with their methods perfected during the war, where they had successfully completed several near impossible missions. Though, in India there was a well established and efficiently run department of investigations, known as C I D, to report on sensitive state related affairs and the C I D had extensive dossiers on political leaders of all colours. However, their methods were traditional and almost outdated. Attlee accepted the need for the specialised intelligence units, and right away issued orders to relocate several such units to India. To maintain the rigid secrecy, the intelligence units were moved to India on different dates. Their existence and whereabouts were known only to the Viceroy and his Chief of Staff. The best of the lot were sent to Delhi and Bombay.

Nehru

From the moment Mountbatten landed at Delhi's Palam airport on March 22, 1947, he began to act according to a script written during the days he was preparing for the role of the Indian Viceroy. With the departure of the deliberately humiliated Wavell, whose humiliation had made everyone in the Congress happy, he earnestly took the job of charming the Congress bosses. Though all the top Congress leaders were in the aim, his main target was Nehru, because after Gandhi, he was the most important man in the Congress and probably the most vulnerable to Mountbatten's charm. By influencing Nehru, the he hoped to accomplish many difficult tasks.

Nehru, scion of a wealthy high caste Hindu family, was reared at Harrow and Trinity of England. By the time he returned to India, "He was an Englishman in Indian skin".[113] and remained so for the rest of his life. He had a weakness for things that were English, be it cigarettes or wine. Once, in the presence of Gandhi he confessed: "I took sherry (a kind of wine) last evening". [114] It pained Gandhi to once remark: "Jawahar wants Englishmen to go but *Angreziat* (English culture) to stay."[101] Indeed, there remained a kind of wall of *Angreziat* between Nehru and the masses of India, and neither of them could ever cross it. Untimely death of his wife Kamla had made him a lonely person. He once wrote in his letter form a British Jail, "For nearly 26 months...I had not seen a woman even from a distance...what are women like? How do they work? How do they talk and sit and walk?"[115] When Edwina Mountbatten came to India as a glamorous vicereine, Nehru, a widower of 12 years, was ripe for feminine influence

Plan Seduction

While Mountbatten was busy using his charm and position to seduce the Congress leaders, none of it was used for the Muslim League leaders. The relationship that developed between Mountbatten and Jinnah was cold as ice, and the impolite language which the Viceroy used for the Muslim leader was most unusual and intriguing, because it came from a highly polished member of the British royal family. Mountbatten used to call Jinnah an "evil genius" a "psychopathic" case and a "lunatic". Once he even called him a "bastard"[116]

It was all a part of a well conceived plan, in which foul language and apparently frosty relations were to be maintained with the Muslim league leaders to confuse and keep the Congress in false confidence. Offensive language for Jinnah was deliberately used in the presence of the Indian staffs of the Viceroy, who were known to be friendly with those Congress leaders, who were soon going to rule India.[117] For a long time to come the Congress could not realise that under the camouflage of abuse, solid work was being done for the creation of Pakistan, and when it came to know it was too late. This plan served one more purpose; it showed the world that Britain had earnestly tried to leave a united India. It was the obstinacy of that 'lunatic' Jinnah which had compelled them to accept the partition, and their Viceroy was really a sad figure when he most reluctantly divided India. Mountbatten maintained that the partition was sheer madness and once said: "The responsibility for this mad decision must be placed squarely on Indian shoulders in the eyes of the world". [118] Under the canopy of this white lie, the Imperial Government of Britain could also say that the holocaust of partition was not its creation and India was divided because Jinnah was "a psychopathic case, hell bent on this Pakistan."[119]

Edwina Mountbatten

The Viceroy's house was not new to Edwina, for once before she had stayed there as the guest of Lord Reading, the Viceroy of India. She, a charming lady of 21, was then known as Edwina Ashley, which was her maiden name. She had accompanied the large party of the Prince of Wales Edward, the eldest son of King George V and the future King of England. She herself was from a family of great wealth and position. One of her forefathers was the Earl of Shaftsbury and her grandfather, Sir Ernest Cassel was one of the wealthiest bankers of England. In her life she had been to many royal palaces, but nowhere had she seen so much luxury and opulence. She was amazed when one of her friends whispered that the Viceroy's house had 340 rooms, 37 grand salons and there was a permanent army of 5000 servants to look after the Viceroy's needs and comforts. In this very house, on February 14, 1922, Dicky proposed to her, and Edwina could not refuse the proposal of this tall and handsome man. At that time she was just one of the many guests, but now she was there as Vicereine Edwina Mountbatten, the mistress of the house. Again, an army of 5000 servants was there, waiting for her command, to fulfill all her wishes.

In 1922 Louis Mountbatten married Edwina Ashley, heiress to two million pounds of wealth, and entered a life of luxury, never before seen by him. Louis at that time was a minor naval officer on a paltry monthly salary of 50 pounds and 17 shillings. By a tortuously long and complex relationship he technically could claim to be the great grandson of Queen Victoria. After the marriage for years to come, most of his days and evenings were spent in clubs, polo grounds and theatres, and the remainder in water — skiing, yachting, and frolicking. Edwina's wealth had made all these pursuits possible. She herself could be spotted fluttering like a colourful social butterfly busy in claiming her territory, which stretched from London to Paris to the Riviera. This was the time when she acquired a lifelong longing for grand gala parties.

As a Vicereine, at last she had the chance of a lifetime to satisfy her craving for parties, for she now had access to unlimited money to entertain her guests. During the days she was Vicereine of India, she hosted party after party. The total number of guests she had invited over these parties were well over 25000,[120] of course with all the expenses paid from the coffers of the Indian Government. Jaya Thadani, Lady-in-waiting to Edwina, recalls: "Everybody was determined to drink the Viceroy's cellar dry."[166]

Mountbattern

During the Second World War, Mountbatten was given the command of an almost new destroyer, HMS Kelly. One morning in May 1941, before the warship could fire its first salvo, it was sent to the bottom of the sea, in a surprise attack by the Stuka dive bombers of the Luftwaffe. Mountbatten survived the attack, but not the shame. After drying his wet white tunic and gathering enougł courage, Mountbatten appeared before the Prime Minister with a request for the command of a second warship. Winston Churchill, who had the complete action report of the HMS Kelly, was visibly annoyed, and his retort became a famous quote: "What could you hope to achieve except to be sunk in a bigger and more expensive ship this time?" As a punishment, Mountbatten was grounded for the next two and a half years to push files. His break came in October 1943, when he was appointed as the Supreme Allied Commander of South East Asia, "prompting complaints of nepotism against his cousin the king."[173] This time he got lucky, because there America was fighting a sort of personal war with Japan, with whom she had a score to settle for attacking Pearl Harbour. On 6th August, a B-29 bomber dropped an atomic bomb on Hiroshima, and three days later another bomb was dropped on Nagasaki. The very next day, on 10th August, Japan announced her unconditional surrender to America. Seizing the opportunity, Mountbatten raced to the victory stand, piggy riding on the shoulders of Uncle Sam, and on August 15, 1945, took the surrender of the local Japanese army units, whose Supreme Commander in Japan had already surrendered to America, several days before. The event was prominently reported by a section of the British press, projecting as if Japan had surrendered to Mountbatten and not to America. He was made a war hero, and when he returned to Britain in May 1946, he was welcomed like one of them.

Edwina

The relationship that developed between the Mountbattens and Nehru, the interim Prime Minister of India, was noticed by many. Both, Indian and foreign writers have written about their relationship. Some made only passing comments, while the others have described it in detail. Writers like Durga Das have made small comments like "Nehru himself had developed a measure of intimacy with both, Lord and Lady Mountbatten..."[121] or quoted Sardar Patel "... Nehru was unduly amenable to Mountbatten's influence".[122] Some writers commented : "Often, over tea, a stroll in the Mughal Gardens, or a swim in the viceregal pool, she had been able to charm Nehru out of his gloom, redress a situation and subtly encourage her husband's efforts"[123]. Lawrence James, a reputed British historian, found that Edwina Mountbatten "was a jejune socialite with a record for infidelity, which her husband appears to have overlooked". He further adds: "the vicereine became infatuated with Nehru. This was a disastrous intrusion of private passion into public life, since their flirtations were observed". He was candid enough to remark: '...to judge from what is known of the love letters that passed between them, her feelings for the older, wiser widower were those of a school girl with a crush".[124] The love letters were carefully preserved by both of them. When Edwina died on February 21, 1960, of a massive heart attack, she was reading one of these love letters. Even today these are in the possession of their families.

The memories of love lingered. It became a sort of ritual for both of them to meet at least twice a year, with Nehru going to Broadlands, the country house of Edwina in England, and Edwina staying with Nehru in Teen Murti house at New Delhi.[125] When Edwina died, Nehru made members of Indian parliament stand for a minute in her memory. A white flower wreath was specially flown to England from India which was carried by the Indian Navy frigate *Trishul* to the sea burial site of Edwina, as his parting gesture.

Many have speculated to explain the reasons for Edwina to have such a 'record for infidelity' which was 'overlooked' [124] by her husband. To start with, it could have been the wealth of Edwina on which her husband was so dependent. Mountbatten, later on in life, developed friendly relations with many politicians and members of parliament. He was especially close to Tom Driberg, a member of parliament from Labour Party, who was publicly known to be a homosexual. This MP had surmised that his friend Mountbatten was also a homosexual.[126] This could also be one of the reasons, which was further compounded by the unhappy childhood of Edwina, who had lost her mother when she was a child. Her father remarried and her stepmother promptly packed off Edwina to a boarding school. The family's unlimited affluence could never heal the mental trauma, and the psychological scar remained for the rest of her life.

Infidelity of Edwina gave tremendous power to the mellifluous Mountbattens. They were not only able to keep India in the British Commonwealth, but all the British monuments also remained intact and the statues of the English rulers kept standing proudly to remind Indians of their days of slavery. Out of these, one was a 50-feet tall marble statue of King George V, near the India Gate. Even after the last English ruler had left, the memory and the glory of the King remained in India. The memory was intact in the statue and the glory was alive in the song, Jana Gana

Mana. For decades, no one dared to touch the tall statue of George, and only after Nehru it was moved to the Coronation Park of Model Town, Delhi. But the song remained and that song still is the National Anthem of India.

In a few days, India was going to get her long awaited freedom, and those were the days to rejoice, but the joy was marred by some strange rumours. It was suggested that the song, which millions were singing for decades, was difficult to sing. Some also tried to tell the people, who knew Vande Mataram by heart that the song was difficult to remember. The song, which was integral part of the freedom movement, which significantly had helped India to get her freedom, was now claimed to be not good enough to be her national anthem. Sympathisers of the British Raj, one of them was James H. Cousins, the principal of Madanapalle's Theosophical College, advocated in favour of Jana Gana Mana, and eventually it was accepted, ignoring the fact that Kashmir, the home state of Nehru, was missing from the song.

Louis Mountbatten

The lifeline of the island nation Britain passed through the sea, and the navy was the protector of that line. Whether it was the Invincible Armada of Spain or the menacing warships of Napoleon or the destructive U Boats of Hitler, it always was the navy which came forward to save that lifeline. Britain rightly became proud of her navy, and loved to decorate her naval officers with multi-coloured ribbons and glittering trinkets. As a result, many in ceremonial dresses looked like walking Christmas trees. Mountbatten was no exception. Indian politicians and princes were both, almost equally, impressed by this walking colourful tree.

Mountbatten was fairly successful with his plan seduction. He was in Delhi for a month only and had already made a progress in his mission. Events were happening to his entire satisfaction, but one hurdle remained, and that was the partition of India which was still far away. This was a very peculiar situation in which Britain wanted to partition India, but could not openly advocate it. The work was to be done with utmost tact and under the cover of secrecy, for it was to be shown to the world that Britain was agreeing to the partition of India under great compulsion, and that they tried all the tact that was within their power, to avoid the division. It was only because Jinnah and his Muslim League were hell bent upon Pakistan, and the Congress had agreed to it, they, very reluctantly and with a sad heart, had to agree to the partition.

On the basis of new research, it can now be claimed that Britain had lost her confidence in Gandhi, after his Quit India call. By 1946, the political leaders at Westminster had concluded that it would not be prudent for them to depend on an independent India ruled by the Congress of Gandhi and Nehru. They strongly suspected that the new nation would not support the Western interests in containing the possible advance by Soviet Russia of Stalin; therefore they favoured the creation of Pakistan, to serve the Western strategic interests.[112] They were correct in their assessment. Gandhi died, so no one could ever know about his plans for the future, but Nehru did favour Russia; even at the cost of jeopardising India's relations with the West.

There were three parties involved in the division of India. First was the Muslim League. The demand had initially originated from them, and they wanted to divide India as soon as it was possible. Second was Britain, and they too wanted the partition for which they had their own reasons, but because of the world opinion were under the compulsion to act as if they wanted to leave India intact in one piece. Their Viceroy had once declared: "No one could ever induce me to agree for partition, but this fantastic communal madness leaves no other course open to me". He further added; "In the eyes of the world, the responsibility for this decision must be squarely placed on Indian shoulders"[118]. In fact Mountbatten wanted to eat the cake and have it too. The third party was the Congress. This mammoth party had numerous leaders, but actually was under the control of four; they were Gandhi, Patel, Nehru and Prasad. Though all of them wanted a united India, but only Gandhi was as adamant to see India united as his political foe, Jinnah, wanted to divide it. Gandhi had declared in his prayer meetings that India could be divided only over his dead body, and in a reply, Jinnah vowed to "divide India or destroy India". Mountbatten was aware of the great moral force of Mahatma, who was also the undisputed leader of the masses, and without his consent, India could never be divided. The Viceroy also found, and found correctly, that the Congress leadership was too old and too tired to carry on the fight for independence any further, and if they were handled properly, they might agree to the division of India.

19

Plan Balkan — A Bogus Document

It Divided India

The summer of the year 1947 was unusually hot. There was an area of depression somewhere in the south of Delhi, and the hot air that came blowing from the Thar Desert, converted Delhi into a furnace. Everyone was oppressed by the heat except the Viceroy, because he had imported three air conditioners — for the first time in Delhi — from the United States, to make the infamous Indian summer, bearable.

The British Raj had built at Simla, a spacious grand lodge for her Viceroys, where they traditionally used to cocoon themselves during the five Indian summer months. Mountbatten, protected by the cool of the air conditioners, decided to ignore the tradition and stayed on at Delhi, because from Simla, it was not possible to keep a close contact with Indian politicians and a close watch over Indian politics.

There was some thing in the Indian air. Whoever came to India, be it untamed Sakas or barbaric Huns or rustic

Muslims, all were soon mellowed by the luxurious Indian climate and the easy way of life. The Englishmen were no exception. Back in England they were known as Nabobs—adapted from the word Nawabs, who were famous for their idle life of luxury—for their rich and leisurely life, and the Mountbattens also proved to be the same. They enjoyed their mornings on the backs of a pair of stallion, trotting on the roads of many villages that surrounded Delhi of that time. While some of the evenings were kept for a leisurely stroll in the fragrant gardens attached to the house, the rest were kept for frolicking in the cool of the viceregal pool. Nights were invariably reserved for parties. It was customary for Indian Viceroys to frequently host brilliant balls, whether they were at Simla for the five summer months or were in Delhi, for the remainder of the year. At these grand feasts, the guests were European, wines were European, crockery and cutlery too were European, even the menus were always European, only waiters and money were not European, these two were invariably Indian. What better use could there ever be for the money paid in taxes by the poor Indians?

It was the last week of April and Mountbatten still had fourteen months time for the deadline of June 1948, the publicly announced date by which Britain was to vacate India. There was no hurry in the moves and no urgency in Mountbatten's actions, but all this was to soon change after the visit of a man from Bombay. Mountbatten had requested Attlee for Special Intelligence Teams (SIT) and several were sent to India. The members of SIT, trained during the Second World War, were masters of their craft. They worked so independently that even the local CID unit was not aware of their existence. On the orders of the government, they had come a month before the Mountbattens arrived at Delhi. The SIT of Bombay stumbled upon a secret so important that the unit-chief decided to report in person. He had brought an large brown envelope with him; it had to be large because it contained a twelve by fifteen inches X-Ray film, along with other documents and photographs.

Some time back SIT, stationed at Bombay, had noticed Jinnah making repeated visits to Dr. J.A.L. Patel, a physician at Bombay. On investigation, it was found that Patel was entrusted with the health of Mr. Jinnah. When Jinnah's own well-being was involved, the man to be trusted was not a Muslim doctor, there were many, but a Hindu. True to the trust, this Hindu never revealed the secret of his patient, had he, the history of the Indian subcontinent would have been different. Intrigued by Jinnah's frequent visits, SIT decided to clandestinely visit the consulting Chamber of Dr. Patel, and the information they found was soon to affect the lives of millions of Indians. The doctor had several chest X-Rays of Jinnah, the first was about a year old. He had diagnosed that his patient was suffering from the pulmonary tuberculosis.

In 1947, no specific treatment for tuberculosis was available in India, and doctors were treating their tubercular patients with useless and ineffective preparations and tonics. Those who could afford it were sent to T.B. sanatoriums, where they were left to slowly die. Kamala, wife of Jawaharlal Nehru, was one of them. Streptomycin, the first effective antibiotic in the treatment of tuberculosis was discovered way back in 1944, and was put to use by 1945, but that was wartime and the antibiotic was made available for civilian use only towards the end of 1946. It reached Indian cities only towards the end of 1950. Jinnah was now a man who was condemned to slowly die, and the countdown had started with the diagnosis of tuberculosis.

SIT picked an X-Ray from the collection of Dr. Patel, with the hope that the doctor would never notice the missing plate. He never did. SIT also photographed the entire case sheet and a detailed report, to be submitted to the Viceroy, was prepared.

Mountbatten took a long time to read the report, and by the time he finished, he was a changed man. The ease and leisure disappeared from his actions, and now he was a man in a hurry. He was certain if Jinnah died before the partition of India, his hope to divide the people too would forever be buried along with the dead body of the Muslim leader. After Jinnah there was none capable enough to take charge of the Muslim community, and so the demand for Pakistan would have died along with him. Alarmed, Mountbatten called for an immediate meeting of the British medical specialists stationed at Delhi, and asked them to comment on the health and prognosis of the person, whose medical case sheet and X-Ray film they were shown; of course without disclosing the identity of the patient.

X-Ray was discovered by Wilhelm Roentgen, a German scientist, in 1895. Techniques of its use were slowly refined, and by 1920, it became a well accepted tool in the hands of medical men. Nowadays whenever an X-Ray is taken, intensifying screens are invariably used, which are a pair of specially coated plastic plates. During the procedure, X-Ray film is sandwiched between the intensifying screens, which glow brightly on exposure and increase the photographic-effect manifold on the film, resulting in a clear picture of high quality definition. In 1946, when Jinnah's X-Ray was taken, intensifying screens were not in use. It was customary to do non-intensifying screen study, in which the X-Ray film alone was placed in a lightproof paper envelope. As a result very long exposures were required; still the quality was invariably poor.

The X-Ray of Jinnah showed two circular white patches in his lung. Because it was not known at that time a diagnosis of tuberculosis shouldn't be made on the basis of X-Ray alone, Jinnah was declared a tubercular patient. Only later it was clear that other conditions could also mimic a similar picture on an X-Ray, such as lung cancer, sarcoidosis and fungal infections of the lung; even today, with the sophisticated equipment and the highly refined techniques, it is not possible to make a confirmed diagnosis of the tuberculosis, on the basis of X-Ray study alone.

At the meeting called by Mountbatten, the opinion of the medical specialists was divided. While some agreed with Dr. Patel's diagnosis, others were of the belief that the patient was suffering from lung cancer [See footnote], but all of them were of the view that the patient was a man — female's breasts cast shadows — well into his sixties — X-Ray visible union of breast bones occurs during the sixties. They also pronounced that the man was either bedridden or soon would be, and gave him no more than six more months to live. True to the medical prediction, Jinnah was 70 years old, and was soon confined to the bed, never to walk again, though he lived much longer than the predicted six; he lived for sixteen more months. For his last days, he was shifted to a sanatorium at Ziarat in Pakistan, where he finally succumbed to death on September 11, 1948. Officially he died of pulmonary tuberculosis, but most probably it was the carcinoma of the lung which killed him.

The treatment suggested by the medical experts, was Lobotomy — an operation of the lung in which the diseased portion is surgically removed —along with a course of streptomycin by intramuscular injections. The experts argued that if the disease was tuberculosis the treatment might cure him, and in case it was cancer, the operation might add more months to the life of that man. At that time Delhi had both, the streptomycin injections and the facility for an operation. Americans had created a modern medical facility at the Safdarjang Hospital — at that time known as American Hospital — for the Second World War soldiers, and the British had their own Willingdon Hospital — presently known as Ram Manohar Lohia — with all the modern medical facilities. One word from Mountbatten and Jinnah's life could have been saved, or at least prolonged.

The Viceroy was in a dilemma. If he helped, the secret of Jinnah would have been out and known to everyone, including the Congress, and if not, the Muslim League leader would die early. After days of deliberation and a few restless nights, Mountbatten decided to let the secret remain a secret, and no mention of it was ever made in the official papers. For Britain, the creation of Pakistan was far more important than the life of Jinnah.

Mountbatten maintained a claim that he never knew about Jinnah's disease. In the official records, even a small hint was never made about his falling health,[128] as if the Viceroy had developed a kind of blindness, and was unable to see what his predecessor had clearly seen. Lord Wavell had noted in his diary on January 10, 1947, that Jinnah was 'a sick man'. The sick man became sicker and in the same diary on 28th Feb 1947, the illness was again noted[128]. Mountbatten was a "very meticulous man" [129] and retained a "most extensive collection of documents and papers"[129] relating to the period of his Viceroyalty. Jinnah was ill, but the fact was never mentioned by Mountbatten in any of his records. He never gave "any hint that Jinnah was a dying man", [128] obviously his aim was never to divulge the secret of Jinnah.

Note: — *Most Indian and Pakistani historians have described Jinnah's disease as pulmonary tuberculosis, a few even as a mysterious disease. Lawrence James, an eminent British historian, is of the opinion that Jinnah suffered from 'terminal lung cancer.'*[127]

Division of India

When medical experts gave Jinnah only six more months of life, Mountbatten was stunned, because the death would have ruined all his carefully prepared plans, and British history would have recorded him a failed man. The road map for the independence of India was already drawn and approved by the cabinet. Mountbatten was not authorised to make any changes, but he was desperate and decided to alter it on his own, because getting the official approval for the change would have taken several weeks. He also feared that the secret of Jinnah's illness might be leaked out, any day.

Several months ago, the initial blueprint of a plan to divide India into several small fragments was drawn and it was named 'Plan Balkan.' This name came into prominence during the First World War, and was associated with the fragmentation and elimination of the many nations of that time. This unusual name of the plan was personally chosen by Mountbatten, for its psychologically intimidating nature. In plan Balkan, all the princely states of India — the total number was 565 — were given the right to decide their own future. They could join Hindu India or Muslim Pakistan or remain unattached to independently decide their own future. Provinces of British India were also given the same option. Plan Balkan was a recipe for anarchy[131], because the plan would have divided India not into two, but fragmented her into several dozens of pieces, each with its own independent administration and army. If the Englishmen so far governed India by their *divide and rule* policy, through Balkan they intended to leave India by *fragment and quit* plan. The fragments were to be so insignificant that individually each would have been unable to provide a decent administration to its inhabitants.

Mountbatten decided to make use of the plan Balkan, which he had prepared several months before for such an eventuality. For the success of the plan, it was essential to move Nehru away from his colleagues. At Delhi the plan could have failed, for there were Gandhi and Sardar, who would have seen though the deception, so the Mountbattens, using their charm, persuaded Nehru to spend a few nights with them at Simla, ostensibly to spend a few days away from the monotony of Delhi. To isolate, Nehru was invited alone. Krishna Menon 'served as his Alsatian'[130] and faithfully accompanied him almost everywhere. This time also he went to Simla, along with Nehru.

Englishmen were fanatically attached to their Raj of India, and at times acted ludicrously in safeguarding its interests. One of the Viceroys — Linlithgow in 1942 — imprisoned Nehru. The very next one —Wavell in 1945 — allowed him to go free, and now one of them — Mountbatten in 1947 — was prepared to offer Nehru his best bedroom. Three Viceroys and three seemingly contradictory acts, but in fact all three were safeguarding the interests of the Empire. The passage for Nehru from a British jail to the bedroom of a British Viceroy was the result of their loyalty to the Crown.

After learning of Jinnah's illness, Mountbatten was a man in a hurry, still, like a skilled strategist, he allowed Nehru to relax in the luxury of the viceregal lodge and the salubrious climate of Simla. Like a predator he waited for the right moment before pouncing, for he wanted his prey to be unsuspecting.

One fine evening, when Nehru had some wine and dinner was over, Mountbatten casually handed over a document in a large envelope, and asked him to take it and read it in the privacy of his bedroom. Mountbatten further added that he was showing this yet undisclosed plan to Nehru alone because he regarded him a close friend, who was also a very prominent Congress figure, and he had a feeling that Nehru's response would reflect the reaction of the Congress Party to it. Nehru felt flattered by the importance given to him by the Viceroy of India. It never occurred to him that the Viceroy was acting most improperly, because Mountbatten had no right to disclose to Nehru alone a secret government plan. If he honestly wanted to know the reaction of the Congress Party, he should have consulted Nehru at Delhi, where the opinions of other equally important Congress leaders were available. Moreover to maintain impartiality, the leaders of the Muslim League should also have been informed and asked to comment on the plan.

Though Mountbatten was a Viceroy, he was still an employee of the Crown, and was paid a monthly salary for his services which could be terminated at the sweet will of a man sitting in Westminster. His brief gave him some leeway in negotiations, but 'Attlee always remained the master and Viceroy his servant'[140]. It was not that Mountbatten was not aware of the fact, but the illness of Jinnah came like a bolt from the blue and took him by utter surprise. Now, only one option was left open for him, and risking his career, he took it. Had Nehru cried foul, he would have been sacked. To the great relief of the Viceroy, Nehru, who was a mature and wise politician but an apprentice in statecraft and diplomacy, quietly accepted the plan Balkan as the real truth. The Mountbatten's aim was to isolate Nehru from the main-body of the Congress, and then intimidate him with the horrifying plan Balkan. He expected Nehru to strongly oppose the plan and this was exactly what happened. An agitated Nehru informed the Viceroy that the plan Balkan would be rejected outright by the Congress.

To a much disturbed Nehru, the Viceroy subtly promised to draft another plan, the plan which the British government had originally drawn but feared rejection by the Congress, for it provided for the division of India into two separate nations. Mahatma Gandhi had declared that India could only be divided "over my dead body. So long as I am alive, I will never agree to the partition of India."[133] So far in the Congress, it always was the will of the Mahatma which had prevailed; but from now onwards, it was going to change.

Mountbatten went through the act of drafting a new plan. To help him, he selected an Indian, Bahadur Vapal Pangunni Menon, popularly known as V. P. Menon. He was a self-taught man, without any formal education, who eventually became the Reforms Commissioner. His proximity to the Congress leaders, especially to Sardar, was well known. Mountbatten entrusted the drafting of the plan to V.P. Menon with the hope that the events at Simla would he leaked to the Congress stalwarts at Delhi; some thing which would not have been possible, had he sought the assistance of a British officer. Menon did keep Patel informed of the developments at Simla[134]. Nehru, a novice in the intrigues and intricacies of statecraft, accepted the new plan, for it divided India not into dozens of pieces but only into two, by providing for a Muslim nation, to be carved out of India. Mountbatten first horrified Nehru with the bogus Balkan plan, and then presented, as an alternative, the original British plan which was promptly accepted.

One hundred and ninety years ago, the foundation of British Raj was laid with the help of a fake document, when Robert Clive was preparing for an attack on Siraj-ud-Daula, the Nawab of Bengal. The success of the attack depended on the support of Bengal's wealthy merchants, and to get the cooperation of an Indian merchant named Omichand, the wily Clive crafted a bogus document by forging the signature of Admiral Charles Watson[165]. It was May 1757, when that bogus document was used to establish the British Raj in India. Now, once again, it was the same month of May when in 1947, one more bogus document was used by Mountbatten to ensure the cooperation of yet another Indian, a politician named Nehru, to dismantle the same Raj. The British Raj was established in India on the support of a bogus document, and dismantled with the aid of another bogus document.

As a result of the leak to Sardar by V.P. Menon, the Congress had an idea of the plan for the partition of India. When no outright cry for rejection for the plan came from the Congress, Mountbatten knew that he could now divide India. After securing the firm commitment from Nehru, a vastly pleased Mountbatten at once returned to Delhi. The traditional stay of five months at Simla was reduced to eleven days. It had to, for Jinnah was terminally ill. Without wasting any time, the very next day, on May14, Mountbatten flew to London in his Lancaster, to show his boss the good work done by him. Now only the final nod of Westminister was needed before the plan could be implemented.

Changes in the plan for the independence of India were readily accepted by Attlee and when Mountbatten suggested to him to advance the date of independence by about ten months, it too was approved. The final date for the transfer of power was advanced from June 1948 to August 15, 1947. This date was selected in the memory of the surrender of the local Japanese fighting units to Mountbatten on August 15, 1945. Mountbatten knew that by advancing the date, be would have to adhere to a dangerously unrealistic time table, which was sure to result in hardships and a very heavy loss of Indian lives. He also knew that the political leadership of India would press him to change the date of independence.

In London, the date decided for the independence of India was not made public, and when Mountbatten returned to India, then also no one was given an inkling about the date. On June 2, 1947, the Indian Viceroy, Lord Mountbatten, himself officially announced the date. As soon as the date of 15th August was made public, there were requests to change it, but Mountbatten refused all of them, because he had publicly committed the government and it was not possible to change the date so fixed. India was set to be partitioned into two parts without even starting the process to demarcate their thousands of miles long boundaries. Their financial assets, serving civil and military personnel — running into millions — were also to be divided. It was expected that a very big part of the population would move from one part of India to the other, but there was no plan or government machinery to oversee it. Mountbatten had just 73 days and in the stipulated time, this enormous task was to be somehow completed. India was partitioned and the power was handed over in an indecent and avoidable hurry. Predictably the result was disastrous, and at least one million were either killed or succumbed to the hardships of migration,[136] and thirteen million became homeless.

Because of Jinnah's illness everyone was in a hurry, and it was evident everywhere. Attlee and his cabinet rubber stamped the vice-regal plan, and when the time came for its implementation, the requisite legislation was rushed through Parliament in three days.[137] The House of Lords, dominated by Churchill's Conservative Party, gave the requisite consent without any interference. During the perfunctory passage of the Indian Independence Bill in the House of Commons, Churchill, even though he was the leader of the opposition, did not even enter the Parliament lest he might start a debate and delay the bill. He knew that Pakistan would remain a dream, if the Muslim leader died before the partition of India. Philip Noel-Baker, the Secretary of State for Commonwealth Relations, piloted the Bill through the House of Commons. He recalled: "One day he (Churchill) came in (the House of Commons) and I thought trouble was in store. But he just glared at me and went away".[135]

While Nehru was preparing to be the Prime Minister, and giving final touches to his famous "Tryst with destiny" oration, Indian women were being raped in tens of thousands and their innocent infants were trampled. All the routes from Lahore to Ludhiana were choked with fleeing humanity, and the roads to Amritsar were littered with decaying corpses. The whole process of getting independence was indecently hastened up and clumsily messed up, as a result six million Indians became homeless and six hundred thousand were brutally killed. In Pakistan also, the situation was as appalling as it was in India.

Noted historian Lawrence James writes; "Field Marshal Montgomery expressed his displeasure with how Mountbatten had wound up the Raj. *He made a mess of things. I will write and tell him*". As early as August 10, Ismay (General Lord Ismay) had been disturbed by how events were turning out. He wrote to his wife that the British were departing from India "*with all our good work destroyed and leaving behind anarchy and misery and measureless slaughter*". Two months afterwards, he had come to believe that Mountbatten had failed to show that quintessential viceregal quality—impartiality'[138]

Mountbatten made a "nonsense claim that only 2,00,000 killed, while at least a million lost their lives"[139]. He had the cheek to justify the Indian casualties as normal in an event like this. Had only one tenth Englishmen been killed by a similar act of his, he would have been stripped naked of all his honours, and hanged to death by the British people.

In any other part of the free world, the political blunder committed by Nehru, would have ensured his political death by the vote giving people, but paradoxically the people of India kept loving him and this love made him stronger than any of the many kings who had ever ruled from the power capital of India — Delhi. The secret of it was revealed by an ordinary peasant who had come to Delhi on August 15, 1947. When he was asked by a press reporter: "what have you come to Delhi for?" Revealing the rustic rural wisdom, he replied: "To have the darshan (sight of a venerated person) of Raja Jawaharlal". [141]

'Raja Jawaharlal' of that simple village dweller was the symbol of the return of the Indian's rule, for which all had waited patiently, enduring insults and humiliations for long years. On that day of August, with the return of their rule, the wait was over. Their dream had at last became a reality, and Jawahar was the proof of it. He was the living symbol of the revival of their rule, and the love of the masses, bordering worship, was for that symbol.

20

Song of Slaves Becomes the National Anthem

Backdoor Entry of Jana Gana Mana

It was the night of 14th August. A new nation was going to be born, but the father was missing. Actually he was nowhere to be seěn in the Council House, where the Constituent Assembly, as the provisional Parliament, was going to take charge of the newborn at midnight of 14/15 August. That unhappy father of the nation was Mahatma Gandhi. As a matter of fact he was not even in town. Disgusted, he had exiled himself to Calcutta.

Immediately after the birth of the new nation, Mrs Sucheta Kriplani—who later on became the first woman Chief Minister of U P—was asked, by some unknown, to sing Jana Gana Mana, and this was the occasion, when it was sung for the first time, at an official function of free India.

Mountbatten became the Governor General of India and Nehru the first Prime Minister. The members of the first Cabinet were:

1. Jawaharlal Nehru—Prime minister, External and Commonwealth Relations and Scientific Research.

2. Sardar Patel—Home, Information and Broadcasting and States.
3. Rajendra Prasad—Food and Agriculture.
4. Maulana Azad—Education.
5. John Mathai—Railways and Transport.
6. Sardar Baldev Singh—Defence.
7. Jagjivan Ram—Labour.
8. C.H. Bhabba—Commerce.
9. R.A. Kidwai—Communications.
10. Rajkumari Amrit Kaur—Health.
11. B.R. Ambedkar—Law.
12. R.K. Sanmukham Chetty—Finance.
13. Shyama Prasad Mukherjee—Supplies.
14. N.V. Gadgil—Works, Mine and power.

The same year in 1947, the Indian delegation to the United Nations was requested to give a copy of the 'National Anthem' of India, so that the orchestra could practise on it. The delegation mysteriously possessed a gramophone record of the song, Jana Gana Mana. The record was handed over to the United Nations orchestra, and subsequently, it was played at a function of the United Nations. It was for the second time that Jana Gana Mana was officially played for India. How the Indian delegation got the gramophone record of Jana Gana Mana only, and who authorised them to pass it on as the national anthem of India, has never been revealed. The use of Jana Gana Mana, on these two occasions, was repeatedly cited to favour it as the national anthem of India. At the time when India was about to get her independence, there were many popular songs full of inspiration and nationalism, but, amazingly, out of all of these, the recorded music of only Jana Gana Mana was available with the Indian delegation to the United Nations.

It was long since evident that the British would be leaving India. As early as February 20, 1947, it was officially confirmed by the British Prime Minister. Still, surprisingly no attempt was made to finalise the choice of the national anthem, as was done in the case of the national flag. Three weeks before India got her independence, on July 22, 1947, Nehru himself brought a flag to the constituent assembly and in a dramatic gesture unfurled it before the entire gathering with these words: "Sir, this is our national flag". After that he moved a resolution "Resolved that the national flag of India shall be a horizontal tricolour of deep saffron (Kesari), white and dark green in equal proportions. In the centre of the white band shall be a wheel in navy blue, to represent the Charkha. The design of the wheel shall be that of the wheel (Chakra) which appears on the abacus of the Sarnath Lion Capital of Asoka..."

A well planned strategy was used to convince the members of the Constituent Assembly of the superiority of the Ashoka Chakra, over the Gandhi Charkha. A year later, the strategy was the same, when on August 25, 1948; the Constituent Assembly was unsuccessfully pleaded to accept Jana Gana Mana as the national anthem of India.

The strategy consisted of three parts.
Part one—Praise
Part two—Imaginary technical fault.
Part three—International consideration.

Praise: Acting on the strategy, Nehru first praised the common man's Charkha. It was the same Charkha which was used by Gandhi, as a powerful weapon against the economic tyranny of Britain. With it, Mahatma Gandhi was able to weaken the strangulating hold of Manchester over the Indian cloth market. The symbol of Charkha was much despised by the English, and they must have rejoiced, when the decision to change it was taken. Nehru said; "I am sure that many in this house will feel the glow and warmth, which I feel at the present moment, for behind this resolution and the flag lies history, the concentrated history of a short span in a nation's existence."[142] Nehru continued with the praise, "We looked up to this flag, not only with pride and enthusiasm but with a tingling in our veins and also how, when we were sometimes down and out, the sight of this flag gave us courage to go on."[142] Nehru concluded the praise by these words, "In the white previously there was the Charkha, which symbolised the common man in India... and which came to us with the message which Mahatma Gandhi delivered".[142]

Technical fault: After the praise was over, a flimsy technical fault was mentioned "...now this particular Charkha symbol has been slightly varied in this flag, not all of it is taken away. Normally speaking, the symbol on one side of the flag should be exactly the same, as on the other side" [142] when Nehru was saying this from the floor of the Constituent Assembly, he was misleading the members, because there were many national flags—they exist even today—which were not exactly the same on both the sides. The stars and stripes of the United States of America has stars on the left upper corner on one side, and on the right upper corner when viewed from the other side. The hammer and sickle on the red flag of the Soviet Union is also not look alike from both sides. Even Pakistan, who got independence along with India, had chosen an asymmetrical crescent and star flag. In spite of the invalidity of the technical fault, Nehru continued: "...there was this practical difficulty. Therefore after considerable thought, we were convinced that this great symbol which enthused the people should remain in a slightly different form, that the wheel should be there and not the rest of the Charkha".[142] In a clever move, the well known and popular Hindustani Charkha was replaced by the, till then unknown, Ashoka wheel. There were many well known and more elegant wheels associated with true Indian culture, but none was selected. A very famous wheel was the Sun Temple Chariot, at Konark.

International consideration: Concluding the arguments, Nehru introduced an international consideration, ignoring the fact that the primary duty of any government is to look for the national aspirations first and any other, including international, last. Nehru labelled the Hindu period in India as "a narrowly national period" and the Buddhist period of Ashoka as "an international period." He said: "Our mind went back to many wheels, but notably to one famous wheel...the one at the top of the Capital of the Asoka Column...for my part, I am exceedingly happy that we have associated with our flag not only this emblem but in a sense the name of Asoka". He continued to advocate the Asoka symbol "...I should like you to remember that the Asokan period was essentially an international period of Indian history. It was not a narrowly national period".[142] The motion regarding the national flag was adopted by the assembly on July 22, 1947, well before India got her independence. On the other hand the selection of the national anthem, even after independence, was kept pending for years, till just one day was left for India to become a sovereign republic on January 26, 1950.

Though the question of the national anthem was not finalised and was left to he decided later on by the Constituent Assembly, Nehru tried to favour Jana Gana Mana and pre-empted the decision on the national anthem. He wrote letters to all the provincial Governors of states, even though Home Minister Sardar Patel was the minister-in-charge of the states. This was admitted by Nehru in a statement made in the Constituent Assembly on August 25, 1948. He said: "I wrote to all the provincial Governors and asked their views about our adopting 'Jana Gana Mana' or any other song as the national anthem. I asked them to consult their Premiers before replying. Every one of these Governors, except one, the Governor of the Central Province, signified their approval of Jana Gana Mana."[143]

Democratic tradition was not followed. The Constituent Assembly was in session and not the members of the assembly but the provincial Governors, appointed by Nehru's Central Government, were asked for their views. Moreover they were asked about their views on Jana Gaṇa Mana only and not on Vande Mataram. In fact the word Vande Mataram was not even mentioned in the letter. The Governors were not given much choice, and they replied as expected. While making his statement, Nehru could see many members nodding their heads in disagreement. Perhaps he thought: 'If a resolution in favour of Jana Gana Mana is moved now, probably it will not be able to muster support from majority of the members', so deviating from the original plan, the motion for the national anthem was not moved on that day. To appease the house, Nehru promised "the question has to be considered by the Constituent Assembly, and it is open to that Assembly to decide as it chooses. It may decide on a completely new song or tune, if such is available",[143] but this lollipop promise was never kept, and, till the last day, on one pretext or the other, the Constituent Assembly was never given a chance to decide on the national anthem. One year and three months later the Constituent Assembly had still not selected the national anthem. Saturday, 26th November, 1949 was the last day of the session before the house was to be adjourned sine die up to a date, to be fixed—before the January 26, 1950—by the President of the Assembly, Dr. Rajendra Prasad. Shri B. Das, a member from Orissa, asked the President: "Sir, I would like to know if you are going to make a pronouncement as to whether Vande Mataram should be the national song and what should be our national anthem?"[144] The matter was still not discussed and once again deferred. The President replied, "I am not going to make any announcement now. That matter will be considered later on, if necessary, by the Assembly when we meet in January"[144]

Even in January, the Assembly was not given an opportunity to deliberate over the issue and select the national anthem of its choice. The intention was to delay the matter, till the very last day and then confront it with a pre-decided choice, without giving the members a chance to debate on the question of the national anthem and let them decide by the majority vote. Someone had calculated that in the rush of the last day events, members would not be able to effectively debate on it, and as the future revealed, this was exactly what happened.

It is to be noted that Jana Gana Mana was the defacto national anthem from August 25, 1948. In a statement given on that day to the Constituent Assembly, Nehru had said, "...the cabinet considered the matter and came to the decision that provisionally 'Jana Gana Mana' should be used as the national anthem, till such time as the Constituent Assembly come to a final decisions. Instructions were issued accordingly to the provincial governments."[143] It was most unusual that the final decision-making body, the Constituent Assembly of India, was informed after the implementation of the decision.

In all these episodes, the position of the Assembly President, Dr. Rajendra Prasad was most precarious. Nehru, as the Prime Minister, was the head of the Cabinet and as such it was his sole prerogative to appoint or dismiss anyone from the post of a Cabinet Minister. Dr. Prasad was the Food and Agriculture Minister, selected on Nehru's invitation. As an informed lawyer, he was well aware that any decision once taken by the Cabinet was regarded as the collective decision of each and every member; even if a member opposed it during the decision-taking process. Constituent Assembly President, Dr. Rajendra Prasad could not say a word against the song, Jana Gana Mana, because as the cabinet minister he was bound by the collective decision of the Cabinet. It was a well established rule, that to openly criticise and disagree with a cabinet decision, a minister must first resign from the cabinet post. Shyama

Prasad Mukherjee was the cabinet minister holding the charge of the Industries and Supplies; when he disagreed with the Nehru government, he first resigned (1951) and only then publicly criticised it.

The decision to install Jana Gana Mana as the national anthem of India was already made, which was evident Nehru stated in the Constituent Assembly: "It is unfortunate that some kind of argument has arisen in between Vande Mataram and Jana Gana Mana. Vande Mataram is obviously and indisputably the premier song of India". The modus operandi was the same, as the one used in the case of the Charkha, which was first praised and then discarded. Praise was the first part of the modus operandi and in praise of Vande Mataram, Nehru said: "Vande Mataram is... with a great historical tradition and intimately connected with our struggle for freedom. That position it is bound to retain and no other song can displace it. It represents the passion and poignancy of that struggle".[143] With this statement, the praise part was over.

The next part of the modus operandi required to somehow find a technical fault and then mount an attack on the basis of that fault. Attacking Vande Mataram, Nehru told the house: "It (Vande Mataram) represents the passion and poignancy of that (freedom) struggle, but perhaps not so much the culmination of it.[143] It was a false argument. If it was true for Vande Mataram—that it represented the struggle for freedom, but not the culmination of it—so it was for the Congress party as well, and if the Congress could continue, why not Vande Mataram? The technical fault invented to discard Vande Mataram was as flimsy as the one found to discredit the Charkha. If the Charkha was asymmetrical; Vande Mataram could not be played by the Western musical instruments. Nehru informed the Constituent Assembly: "It was thought by some people that the Vande Mataram tune, with all its very great attractions and historical background, was not easily suitable for being played by orchestras in foreign countries and there was not enough movement in it"[143]

After the technical fault was over; it was time to introduce the international element, which formed the third part of the modus operandi. Nehru informed the honourable members of the Constituent Assembly "when they (UN Band) played it (Jana Gana Mana) before a large (international) gathering, it was very greatly appreciated and representatives of many nations asked for a musical score of this new tune which struck them as distinctive and dignified...From various countries, we received messages of appreciation and congratulation of this tune, which was considered by experts and others as superior to most of the national anthems they have heard."[143] Most of the Constituent Assembly members were loyal Congress-men or novices, who were hesitant to ask critical questions. Had any one of them asked about the names of the 'many nations' who 'very greatly' appreciated the 'tune', he would have seen a face red with embarrassment, and if anyone of them had asked the identity of the 'experts' who found the song 'superior', he would have been given a list of the friends of the British Empire, whose aim was to perpetuate the glory of the King George, through Jana Gana Mana. No such questions were asked and Nehru continued: "The real significance of the national anthem is more abroad than in the home country." It was not true, because national anthem is defined as 'a patriotic song expressing patriotic sentiments. It stirs a sense of loyalty among citizens of a country and is either governmentally authorised or holds that position in popular feeling'. With this definition, it is clear that international appreciation has nothing to do with the national anthem, and the sole criterion is that it should express patriotic sentiments and stir a sense of loyalty in the people of the country.

On the flimsy technical ground that the tune of Vande Mataram was not suitable to be played by foreign orchestras, the song was denied the due honour of being the national anthem of India. Even this technical stand was proved wrong, when Master Krishna Rav, a noted musician of national fame, presented before the Constituent Assembly a charming rendering of Vande Mataram played on Western musical instruments.[168] He also had a letter written by Mr. C.R. Gardener, an expert on Western music and Director of Music of the Bombay City Police Band. In his letter of October 22, 1948, he wrote: "It (Vande Mataram tune) has a pleasing effect on Western ears and all Europeans I know, who have heard me play it, definitely prefer it to Jana Gana Mana. Jana Gana Mana is jumpy and undignified, in my opinion. It has a bad fault known as Musical Tautology..."[169] In his letter he further added: "In Western notations it (Vande Mataram tune) is so simple to play that it can be rendered effectively by even a mediocre band. This is a great asset one must consider in an anthem, that has to be played 'at sight' by bands at Embassy functions all over the world."[169]

But the government had already decided against Vande Mataram and in spite of all the facts in its favour, the song was denied the honours. Indians were shocked and severely criticised the denial. An opinion poll, conducted by a popular newspaper, showed as many as 80 per cent favouring Vande Mataram.

It is clear that all the arguments against Vande Mataram were invalid, but what is not clear is why of the government was so much against Vande Mataram, a pure nationalist song whose patriotic pedigree was devoid of any doubt. We will never know the exact truth, because all the characters are no longer alive. Moreover, this matter was never openly debated in public. It now can only be surmised, on the basis of the facts available at present.

Nehru and a few of his colleagues in Congress believed that the partition of India was based on absurd principles and sometime in future, when they are reviewed, the illogical doctrine of two nations—India and Pakistan—would be finally discarded. Noted writer M.J.Akbar, in Nehru's biography writes: "Nehru remained convinced that somehow this partition would be reversed." [147] Probably in this belief, Nehru worked towards such an India, where after the reversal of partition, Muslims will not find any symbol to object to, and this could be one of the reasons for discarding Vande Mataram, the song which for long was objected to by the Muslims. This belief may have been due to the fact that Jawaharlal's ancestors migrated from Kashmir to Delhi in the year 1716, when Raj Kaul Nehru was employed by Farrukh Siyar, the Mughal Emperor. From that year onwards, the Nehrus worked for various Muslim rulers, for as many as 140 years; till the upheavals of the 1857 war caught Ganga Dhar Nehru, the grandfather of Jawaharlal Nehru, working as a Kotwal (Head police constable) in Delhi. After being associated with Muslims for fourteen decades, perhaps Nehru had the notion that he could understand them better.

Nehru was convinced that the Hindu fundamentalists would he a threat to the unity of India. He once said: "The danger to India, mark you, is not communism. It is Hindu right-wing communalism,"[148] Nehru had a dislike for Hindu fundamentalists and this could also have been one of the reasons. The foundation of such a belief was probably laid in 1899, when his father, Motilal Nehru was 'excommunicated' by the high-caste Hindus, as a punishment for crossing the high seas and refusing the customary *pooja* for the purification. As a result, the Nehru family was 'socially boycotted'.[149] Jawaharlal at that time was at the impressionable age of ten and this treatment of his family might have left a scar on his tender mind. Forty-eight years later, when he became the Prime Minister of India, he did all that was within his power, to keep the Hindu fundamentalists in check. Though, Vande Mataram was loved by all, still a small faction of Muslims criticised by labelling it as a Hindu song. It could have been the imaginary fear of Nehru that the selection of Vande Mataram as the national anthem would encourage the activities of the Hindu fundamentalists. Such an action becomes even more probable, when we find that Nehru, in his own Congress Party, kept pro-Hindu elements 'under strong check'.[150]

With so many doubts and only a little support, why Jana Gana Mana was selected? If, for any reason, Vande Mataram was not suitable, Indian poets could have been requested to pen an altogether new song, which was patriotic and acceptable, as has been done by many countries, including our neighbour Shri Lanka. It is difficult to apprehend the reason. Could it be that India's leaders did not have enough time to ponder over the issue? It could be, for the country at that time was passing through a critical time. As if the untold miseries associated with the just concluded Second World War were not enough, an avalanche of fresh problems was brought by India's partition, which might have taken up all of their time. The condition of Jawaharlal Nehru, the first prime minister of India, was even worse. He not only had to face the national, but also attend to his own domestic problems, which too were many.

The untimely death of his wife Kamala left him alone to care for his only child, a girl named Indira, who fell in love with Feroze Gandhi, a Parsi, and married him against the wishes of her family. The married life of this Parsi couple bestowed them with two sons, Rajiv in the year 1944, and Sanjay two years later. To make his daughter's family life easy; Nehru in 1946 gifted to Feroze, the managing directorship of *National Herald*, a Lucknow-based newspaper, owned by Nehru, but it could not sweeten their married life. After independence, Indira parted ways with Feroze, and started to live with her Prime Minister father; along with three-year-old Rajiv and a year-old Sanjay.

From the very beginning, Nehru had a dislike for his son-in-law, who in turn never missed an opportunity to embarrass Nehru. Feroze persuaded Nehru to get a Congress ticket, and was elected from Rai Barielly. After Feroze became a member of parliament, a sort of history was created when he, a member of the ruling party, became de facto leader of the opposition. Son-in-law leader of the opposition opposed his father-in-law's Congress government for the rest of this life. Mutual dislike and mistrust between Feroze and himself made Nehru worry about the future of his daughter and grandsons. Academically Indira could not achieve much, and suffered from tuberculosis for which no effective treatment was yet available at Delhi. Wonder drugs streptomycin and INH had still not reached the capital of India. These two drugs became available in Delhi by 1951 and only then could Indira be cured of the disease which had already taken the life of her mother, Kamala Nehru. If Nehru was worried about the future of his daughter, he was scared about the prospects of his two infant grandsons. Their father was a Parsi and he was fearful about their acceptance in Hindu-dominated India.

Most probably it was not a single factor, but a combination of many; for a complex pattern was seen in the handling of the Vande Mataram song, which was — and it still is — a very popular song and loved by all. Only a small anti-Hindu sect of Muslims opposed it. This was the same group which had also demanded a separate nation to live the way they liked, and got their Pakistan. With the creation of this Muslim nation, it was believed that only those would choose to remain in India, who were prepared to live in the brotherhood of love and peace with the majority. They did start living with Hindus with amity, without renewing any of their demands which were to hurt the Hindu sentiments. Yet, without any fresh objection against Vande Mataram, the government selected Jana Gana Mana, as the national anthem. However, when attempts were made to dethrone

Vande Mataram, rebellious resistance was encountered, and when it became clear that for want of majority, Jana Gana Mana could never be elevated to the status of National Anthem by means of a resolution in the Constituent Assembly, a back door entry was planned.

Back Door Entry of Jana Gana Mana

On January 26, 1950, India was to be declared a Sovereign Democratic Republic. The Constitution was almost ready. It had been adopted by the assembly on November 26, 1949, yet it was not complete. It still was not signed by the members and had not yet decided on the National Anthem. It would have been a great embarrassment for the republic to come into existence, without an official National Anthem.

Tuesday, January 24, 1950, was the last working day of the Constituent Assembly, and on this day all the pending work, including the selection of the National Anthem was to be somehow completed. Although it was clear that Jana Gana Mana would never be able to muster the requisite majority to achieve the status of the National Anthem, through a resolution.

Though the Nehru cabinet had already "come to the decision that provisionally Jana Gana Mana should be used as the tune for the National Anthem",[143] the status of the song was still that of a "provisional national anthem". Without the ratification of the Constituent Assembly, it could never be declared as the official anthem of India. How to achieve this seemingly difficult task was a cause for worry. The solution was in the hands of Dr. Rajendra Prasad, the presiding officer of the Constituent Assembly. He was approached and requested to get the cabinet decision implemented. When the matter of National Anthem was initially brought before the assembly on 25th Aug'1948, he too had seen the many heads nodding against Jana Gana

Mana. As a member of the cabinet, Prasad had to support the cabinet decision, but at the same time the true Indian in him could not ignore the Vande Mataram. Not knowing what to do, he was in a dilemma and acutely felt the absence of his long time mentor, but Gandhiji was no longer in this mortal world to help him. His nights became sleepless and days full of tension. Then one morning—when he was meditating, the answer came to him like a divine gift. He would carry out the dictum of the cabinet, but at the same time, his inner voice would also not be ignored. The Republic of India would have not one but two national anthems. Both were already selected, one by the 14 members of the Nehru cabinet, and the other by the 330 million Indians. Probably the two anthems arrangement was not liked by Nehru and his relations with Prasad became bitter, and he started to regard him unsecular. Whenever there was an opportunity, a jibe against him was invariably passed by Nehru; as was done when Prasad participated in the ceremonies of the Somnath Temple or paid homage to the pandits of Varanasi. For five years, on one pretext or the other, this President was not allowed to go out of the country, lest he might say a few unsecular words. Even the death of Rajendra Prasad could not make Nehru forget the bitterness. He not only refused to attend the funeral, but did not even send a wreath, to pay the last homage to the first President of India.

The 24th day of January 1950 dawned on Delhi with a pleasantly cool morning. It was well before 11'oclock, but almost all the members had gathered in the constitution hall. The day was Tuesday and many members had already been to the nearby Hanuman Temple, as was evident by a crimson red tilak on their foreheads. The atmosphere in the hall was the same as always found in a college on the last day of the academic session. Bonhomie was present at every corner, where members were seen exchanging pleasantries, with their friends made over the last few years.

When Dr. Rajendra Prasad called the Constituent Assembly of India to order, it was 11 o'clock. The first item on the agenda was taking the pledge, and signing the register by two members — Sri. R.B. Kumbhar and Dr. Y.S. Parmar — and as soon as this was over, Dr. Prasad took the mike. He was looking confident and there was no hesitancy in his voice when he said: "There is one matter which has been pending for discussion, namely the question of the National Anthem." The moment Dr. Prasad finished his sentence; there was a hushed silence in the hall, as every member was eager to hear about the National Anthem. The President continued: "At one time it was thought that the matter might be brought up before the House and a decision taken by the House by way of a resolution. But it has been felt that, instead of taking a formal decision by means of a resolution, it is better if I make a statement with regard to the National Anthem. Accordingly I make this statement."

"The composition consisting of words and music known as Jana Gana Mana is the National Anthem of India subject to such alterations in the word as the government may authorise as occasion arises."[159] At this point, Rajendra Prasad paused for a moment. No one even noticed, and he continued with his confident and steady voice "and the song Vande Mataram, which has played a historic part in the struggle for Indian freedom, shall be honoured equally with Jana Gana Mana and shall have equal status with it. (applause). I hope this will satisfy the members."[159]

The moment the President of the Constituent Assembly of India uttered the words "... shall have equal status" the Sovereign Democratic Republic of India had two National Anthems, for equal status means equal in all respects, even in name. To be equal, both songs are to be identified as the National Anthems, and if different designations are assigned to them, then equality is not there. The present conception that Jana Gana Mana is the National Anthem of India and

Vande Mataram only a National Song, is wrong, because no such distinction was ever made by the constitutional authorities. It is true that the adoption of the National Anthem was never considered and a resolution was never moved in the Constitutional Assembly, as should have been done, and only a statement was made by Dr. Rajendra Prasad, the President of the Assembly. But if it is postulated that the President of the Constitutional Assembly had no authority to impose the National Anthems on the strength of a statement in the Assembly, India has no National Anthem, and a fresh process has to be started for the valid selection of the Anthem. But if that statement was valid, India has two National Anthems.

The legal brain of Prasad had inserted one more precondition in his statement. He had said: "Vande Mataram...shall be honoured equally with Jana Gana Mana". By his long association with law, he knew that bestowing 'equal status' to Vande Mataram was not enough, because government could accord Vande Mataram an equal status, and then forget it forever. To prevent such a move, he had added that Vande Mataram "...shall be honoured equally with Jana Gana Mana", and with this precondition, the government was now bound to accord equal importance to both the National Anthems. In other words, whenever the Anthems were to be sung or their music played— at official functions, ceremonial public occasions, international gatherings, international athletic events, honouring a head of state— they were to be performed in exactly equal numbers; for half the time one and the other half of the time another anthem was to be played. It could never be more or less with any one of them.

India is not the only country in the world to have two National Anthems. New Zealand also has two National Anthems. One is 'Maori Aotearoa' (God defend New Zealand) and the other is 'God save the Queen.' Both anthems have equal official status.

The Government soon forgot the words of the solemn statement, officially made in the Constituent Assembly, by its president in the presence of the full house. The government never equally honoured Vande Mataram. It not only trespassed its authority but also designated Jana Gana Mana alone as the National Anthem of India. Vande Mataram was assigned a rank lower and an inferior title of the 'national song' was given to it. The queen was made a maid, and for the last fifty-six years, it is the maid that is being honoured as a queen.

It was the wishful thinking of those, who thought that by neglecting Vande Mataram, the song would be slowly forgotten and ultimately die. Star of the eyes and throb of the Indian hearts, Vande Mataram is still as fondly remembered as it ever was. A very interesting event occurred around 2002. That was the 70th anniversary year of the BBC World Service and the service decided to celebrate in a big way. For many years people around the world were curious to know the favourite songs of the world, and BBC with its truly global reach, undertook this gigantic project to find out 'The world's Top Ten' songs. In this unique venture, tens of thousands — to be exact 1,50,000, of the BBC world service listeners — took part from 153 countries and voted for about 7000 different songs.[160] When the news was published,[161] millions of Indians read it with eyes wet with tears of joy. Vande Mataram was second in 'The Worlds Top Ten' list. An Irish song '...triumphed over the Indian patriotic song Vande Mataram by the smallest of margins in a poll of world service listeners.'[160] The smallest margin was not revealed, but the only number that can be called smallest (votes cannot be given in fractions) is 'one' and it could be that Vande Mataram polled just one vote less then the song on the top.

A century ago, members of the British race started to oppress a little song of their slaves, but along with the oppression a miracle happened. The more they oppressed, the stronger the song became, and at last, when they had to leave that slave land, the little song was still alive. It was ironical, that the members of the same race were to now eulogise the same, once oppressed, Vande Mataram in front of the whole world[162]

The most revealing aspect of the poll was that the name of Jana Gana Mana was not to be seen in the list. Jana Gana Mana was never liked by the masses, and this song will never be loved by the Indians. It is high time to change the National Anthem of India. If it is changed, it will not be for the first time that a nation will be doing so. To respect the feelings of the people, many nations have done it, and done it repeatedly. To find an appropriate National Anthem, and keep pace with the changing political climate, the Russians have changed their anthem six times.

Their national anthems were:

(1) The Prayer of Russians (1743);
(2) God Save the Tsar (1833);
(3) Lyrics by poet Konstantin (1917);
(4) The Internationale (1921);
(5) Gimn Sovetskovo Soyuja (1944) (Hymn of the Soviet Union);
(6) Patriotiskaya Pesn (1991) (The Patriotic Song);
(7) Gimn Rossiyskaya Federatsiya (2001) (Hymn of the Russian Federation).

The United States of America has also changed her anthem. In 1931, the present anthem 'The Star Spangled Banner' replaced the old 'My Country 'tis of thee'.

The French have the same profound love for their anthem 'La Marseillaise' as Indians have for Vande Mataram. This favourite song was adopted as the French national anthem in 1795. Jealous of its hold over people, Louis XVII banned it in 1815. The ban — lifted after the July revolution of 1830 — was imposed once again. In the end, bowing to the popular demand, 'La Marseillaise' was at last finally reinstated in 1879, to the status of the national anthem. If the French can, Indians too can do it.

A few Indian Muslims oppose Vande Mataram on the ground that it glorifies and depicts the nation as a mother, while to them portrayal of the state as mother is blasphemy. It is definitely not true because two million Muslims of Sri Lanka feel proud to sing their anthem — "Mother Lanka we worship thee ... Leads us, mother, to fullest freedom" (English translation) — in which they worship their mother-nation. In Indonesia Raya (anthem), which identifies the nation as "... my motherland", 210 million Muslims of Indonesia have also not found anything objectionable in addressing their nation as mother.

The glory of Vande Mataram has been eclipsed for long, by the black shadow of Jana Gana Mana, but no eclipse can last forever. Thousands have willingly sacrificed their lives for the motherland with Vande Mataram on their lips, and millions are prepared to sacrifice, if given the magic strength of a mantra that is Vande Mataram. Long ago, when Charles Perrault wrote the fairytale, *Sleeping Beauty*, he was unaware that centuries later another beauty would be cursed, but Vande Mataram was cursed by the wicked English that one day in 1950, she will die by the stroke of a pen. All were heartbroken, but once again a boon was given, "She will not die but fall into deep sleep. She will sleep for a little over half a century. Then one day she will be awakened by the kiss from an Indian." Today there is not one but over 1000 million of them. Kiss this sleeping beauty to awaken her, and let all the hearts be filled with pure pride and pleasure.

Epilogue

After reading this book, many declared that henceforth they intend not to show any respect for lana Gana Mana. My advice to them, and to all others with similar intentions, is to give due respect to lana Gana Mana, as long as this song is our National Anthem.

India is a vibrant democracy, and in a democracy the collective will of the people is supreme. If enough people have enough love for Vande Mataram, one day it is bound to regain its lost position. But, till then we all have to respect the designated National Anthem.

Bibliography

1. Lawrence James. *Raj:* The *Making and Unmaking of British India*-2001 reprint, 1998 edition; Abacus, London, p.16.
2. (i) Lawrence James. *Raj*: The *Making and Unmaking of British India* -2001 reprint, 1998 edition; Abacus, London, p. 208.
   (ii) M.J. Akbar. *Nehru: The Making of India,* Roli Books, 2002, New Delhi, p. 14.
3. Lawrence James. *Raj: The Making and Unmaking of British India,* 2001 reprint, 1998 edition; Abacus, London, pp. 240, 241.
4. Rudyard Kipling. Departmental Ditties 'One Viceroy Resigns'
5. Lawrence James. *Raj:* The *Making and Unmaking of British India* -2001 reprint 1998 edition; Abacus, London, p. 311.
6. Rudyard Kipling. *'The Ballad of East and West'.*
7. *Congress Varnica.* Official journal of the AICC (I); Vol. 2. No. 12, December 1985, p. 335.
8. Deep Chand Bandhu. *History of the Indian National Congress,* Delhi, 2003, p. 25.
9. *Congress Varnica.* Official Journal of AICC(I); Vol. 2, No.12, December 1985, p. 40.
10. V.D. Mahajan. *Modern Indian History,* 2000, New Delhi, p. 385.
11. Lt. Col. Gautam Sharma and R.K. Murti. *Indian National Songs,* 1998, New Delhi, p. 95.

12. V.D. Mahajan. *British Rule in India and After,* 13th Ed, New Delhi, 1978, p.389.
13. *Congress Varnica.* Official journal of the AICC (I); Vol. 2. No. 12, December 1985, pp.190 to 197.
14. V.D. Mahajan. *Modern Indian History,* 2000, New Delhi, p. 390
15. V.D. Mahajan. *British Rule in India and After,* 13th edition.1978, New Delhi, p. 396.
16. V.D. Mahajan. *British Rule in India and After,* 13th edition.1978, New Delhi, p. 280.
17. *The Bengalee,* Calcutta December 27, 1911(Microfilms provided by the British Library of Newspapers, Colindale, London)
18. Nirad C. Chaudhuri. *Thy Hand,* London 1987, p. 596.
19. Jawaharlal Neḥru. *The Discovery of India,* 9th impression 1989. Oxford University press, p. 297.
20. Krishna Dutta and Andrew Robinson. *Rabindranath Tagore: The Myriad-Minded Man.* Rupa Paperback 2000, New Delhi, p. 20.
21. Krishna Dutta and Andrew Robinson. *Rabindranath Tagore: The Myriad-Minded Man.* Rupa Paperback 2000, New Delhi, p. 352.
22. Krishna Dutta and Andrew Robinson. *Rabindranath Tagore: The Myriad-Minded Man.* Rupa Paperback 2000, New Delhi, p. 19.
23. Krishna Dutta and Andrew Robinson. *Rabindranath Tagore: The Myriad-Minded Man.* Rupa Paperback 2000, New Delhi, p. 20.
24. Krishna Dutta and Andrew Robinson. *Rabindranath Tagore: The Myriad-Minded Man.* Rupa Paperback 2000, New Delhi, p.8.
25. Krishna Dutta and Andrew Robinson *Rabindranath Tagore: The Myriad-Minded Man.* Rupa Paperback 2000, New Delhi, p. 35.
26. W.B. Yeats. *Introduction to 'Gitanjali'.* Macmillan Pocket Tagore edition 1974, New Delhi, p. 7.
27. Mahatma Gandhi. *Young India,* April 13, 1921, p. 477.

28. Barbara T. Gates. *Victorian Suicides: Mad Crimes and Sad Histories,* Princeton University Press-1988. Chapter 5
29. Bayley, C.A. 'From Ritual to Ceremony' in *Mirrors of Mortality: Studies in the Social History of Death,* Ed Joachim Whaley, London, Europa Publications-1981, p. 173.
30. Westermarck, Edward. *Origin and Development of Moral Ideas* Macmillan, 1903, London, p. 242.
31. Lawrence James. *Raj:* The *Making and Unmaking of British India*-2001 reprint 1998 edition; Abacus, London, p. 51.
32. Lawrence James. *Raj:* The *Making and Unmaking of British India* -2001 reprint 1998 edition; Abacus, London, p. 52.
33. Krishna Dutta and Andrew Robinson. *Rabindranath Tagore: The Myriad-Minded Man* Rupa Paperback 2000, New Delhi, p. 88.
34. Rabindranath's poem *'Bibashana'* (without clothes). Written in the year 1885.
35. Krishna Dutta and Andrew Robinson. *Rabindranath Tagore: The Myriad-Minded Man.* Rupa Paperback 2000, New Delhi, p.161.
36. The 640-kg Silver Throne was made by the master craftsmen for the Coronation Durbar. At present it is in the museum of the Rashtrapati Bhawan.
37. Lt. Col. Gautam Sharma and R.K. Murthi. *Indian National Songs.* 1998, New Delhi, p. 38.
38. Lt. Col. Gautam Sharma and R.K. Murthi. *Indian National Songs.*1998, New Delhi, p. 97.
39. *The Bengalee.* Vol. LII No. 302 dated December 27, 1911 (Microfilms provided by the British Library of Newspapers, Colindale, London)
40. *The Bengalee.* Vol. LII No. 303 dated December 28, 1911(Microfilms provided by the British Library of Newspapers, Colindale, London)

41. *The Bengalee.* Vol. LII No. 302 dated December 27, 1911(Microfilms provided by the British Library of Newspapers, Colindale, London), p. 2.
42. Lawrence James. *Raj:* The *Making and Unmaking of British India.* 2001 reprint 1998 edition; Abacus, London, p. 316.
43. Lawrence James. *Raj:* The *Making and Unmaking of British India.* 2001 reprint 1998 edition; Abacus, London, p. 321.
44. Dr. Puttulal Sukla. *Adhunic Hindi-Kavya me Chanda Yojna.* Lucknow, 1958 edition, pp. 295 and 297.
45. Dr. Puttulal Sukla. *Adhunic Hindi-Kavya me Chanda Yojna.* Lucknow, 1958 edition, p. 297.
46. Krishna Dutta and Andrew Robinson. *Rabindranath Tagore: The Myriad-Minded Man.* Rupa Paperback 2000, New Delhi, p. 20.
47. *The Religion of Man,* London (1931) essays, p. 170.
48. Holy Quran, Surah An-Nisa, Para V, Aayat No. 36
49. Holy Quran, Surah An-Nisa, Para V, Aayat No.48
50. (i) Krishna Dutta and Andrew Robinson. *Rabindranath Tagore: The Myriad-Minded Man.* Rupa Paperback 2000, New Delhi, p. 161.

    (ii) Ezra Pound. *The letters of Ezra Pound 1907-1941.* D.D. Paige. London 1951.Ed. p. 49.
51. Brian Lapping. *End of Empire.* St. Martin's Press, New York, 1985, p. 43.
52. *Manchester Guardian.* January 1, 1912. (Microfilms provided by the British Library of Newspapers, Colindale, London)
53. *Manchester Guardian.* January 11, 1912. (Microfilms provided by the British Library of Newspapers, Colindale, London)
54. *The Bengalee,* Calcutta. January30, 1912. (Microfilms provided by The British Library of Newspapers, Colindale, London)

55. Krishna Dutta and Andrew Robinson. *Rabindranath Tagore: The Myriad-Minded Man.* Rupa Paperback 2000, New Delhi, p.165.
56. After Tokyo, London is the second most expensive city in the world.
57. Mary M. Lago. *Imperfect Encounter: Letters of William Rothenstein and Rabindranath* Tagore, *1911-1941.* Cambridge (Massachusetts) 1972. Ed. p. 140.
58. *Congress Varnica.* Official journal of the AICC (I), Vol. 2. No. 12, December 1985, p. 29.
59. Krishna Dutta and Andrew Robinson. *Rabindranath Tagore: The Myriad-Minded Man.* Rupa Paperback 2000, New Delhi, p. 216.
60. Krishna Dutta and Andrew Robinson. *Rabindranath Tagore: The Myriad-Minded Man.* Rupa Paperback 2000, New Delhi, p. 217.
61. *Collected Works of Mahatma Gandhi.* Vol: 28, p. 429.
62. Krishna Dutta and Andrew Robinson. *Rabindranath Tagore: The Myriad-Minded Man.* Rupa Paperback 2000, New Delhi, p. 225.
63. Jag Pravesh Chandlers. *Tagore and Gandhi Argue.* Ed. p. 17.
64. Lt. Col. Gautam Sharma and R.K. Murthi. *Indian National Songs.* 1998, New Delhi, p. 104.
65. W.B. Yeats. *Introduction to 'Gitanjali'.* Macmillan pocket Tagore edition 1974, New Delhi, p. 6.
66. W.B. Yeats. *Introduction to Gitanjali.* Macmillan pocket Tagore edition. 1974, New Delhi, p. 5.
67. W.B.Yeats. *Introduction to Gitanjali.* Macmillan pocket Tagore edition 1974, New Delhi, p. 10.
68. Krishna Dutta and Andrew Robinson. *Rabindranath Tagore: The Myriad-Minded Man* Rupa Paperback 2000, New Delhi, p.43
69. W.B. Yeats. *Introduction to 'Gitanjali',* p. 9.
70. Nowell-Smith. *Letters to Macmillan,* London 1967. Ed., p. 291.
71. Allan Wade. *The letters of W.B. Yeats.* Ed., pp. 834 and 835.

72. Krishna Dutta and Andrew Robinson. *Rabindranath Tagore: The Myriad-Minded Man.* Rupa Paperback 2000, New Delhi, p. 350.
73. Prose Verse I and IV are from *Gitanjali.*
74. Rabindranath. 'Jana Gana Mana'. Verse: 5
75. Nanda, B.R. *Gokhale.* New Delhi.1977, pp. 400 and 401.
76. Official First World War Records. The Military Efforts of the British Empire', available on the internet.
77. (i) V.D. Mahajan. *Modern Indian History,* 2000, New Delhi, p.407.
    (ii) Lawrence James. *Rise and fall of the British Empire,* 1998, Abacus, London, p. 353.
78. Lt. Col. Gautam Sharma and R.K. Murthi. *Indian National Songs* 1998, New Delhi, p. 1.
79. *Cambridge History of India* .Vol IV, p. 608.
80. Lt. Col. Gautam Sharma and R.K. Murthi. *Indian National Songs* 1998, New Delhi, p. 21.
81. Krishna Dutta and Andrew Robinson. *Rabindranath Tagore: The Myriad-Minded Man* Rupa Paperback 2000, New Delhi, p. 179.
82. *Mahayogi,* p.47.
83. *A Book of India,* p. 67.
84. *The First Sixty Years*—Vol-II, p. 577.
85. *Tilak and the Struggle of India's Freedom.*
86. *Glorious Thoughts of Tagore,* p. 165,
87. Lt. Col. Gautam Sharma and R.K. Murthi. *Indian National Songs* 1998, New Delhi., p. 1.
88. Durga Das. *India from Curzon to Nehru and After.* Rupa & Co, New Delhi, 2001, p. 50.
89. Durga Das. *India from Curzon to Nehru and After.* Rupa & Co, New Delhi, 2001, p. 51.
90. Jawaharlal Nehru. *The Discovery of India,* 9th impression Oxford University Press. 1989, p. 346,
91. Durga Das. *India from Curzon to Nehru and After.* Rupa & Co, New Delhi, 2001, p. 51.
92. National Book Trust. *Vishnu Digambar Paluskar,* p. 54.

93. Lt. Col. Gautam Sharma and R.K. Murthi. *Indian National Songs.* 1998 New Delhi, p. 23.
94. M.J. Akbar. *Nehru-The Making of India* March 2003 impression. Roli Books, New Delhi, p. 383.
95. (i) Roberts. *Eminent Churchillians,* pp. 129 to 132.
(ii) Lawrence James. *Raj: The Making and Unmaking of British India*-2001 reprint, 1998 edition; Abacus, London, p. 636.
96. Durga Das. *India from Curzon to Nehru and After,* Rupa & co 2001,New Delhi, p. 636.
97. Winston Churchill in the House of Commons, February 1931.
98. Winston Churchill in a speech at Lord Mayor's banquet, November 10, 1942.
99. Larry Collins and Dominique Lapierre. *Freedom at Midnight,* Vikas 1976, New Delhi, p. 69.
100. H.J. Dolley. 'Great Britain's Last Battle& C' *International History Review.* Vol 11 (1989), p. 493.
101. Durga Das. *India from Curzon to Nehru and After,* Rupa & Co,2001,New Delhi, p. 261.
102. Larry Collins and Dominique Lapierre. *Freedom at Midnight,* Vikas 1976, New Delhi, p. 84.
103. Details of the event can be seen in *India from Curzon to Nehru & After* by Durga Das. Rupa & Co.2001, New Delhi, pp. 231-232.
104. Durga Das. *India from Curzon to Nehru and After* Rupa & Co, 2001, New Delhi. p. 230.
105. Lawrence James. *Raj: The Making and Unmaking of British India* 2001 reprint 1998, edition; Abacus, London, p. 321.
106. Lawrence James. Raj: The Making and Unmaking of British India, 2001 reprint,1998 edition; Abacus, London, p. 589.
107. Deccan Herald, Bangalore, April 27, 1981.
108. Khalikuzzama. *Pathway,* p. 372.

109. Lawrence James. *Raj: The Making and Unmaking of British India,*2001 reprint 1998 edition; Abacus, London, p. 589.
110. Durga Das. *India from Curzon to Nehru and After,* also has similar views, p. 222.
111. Lawrence James. *The Rise and Fall of the British Empire* 1998, Abacus, London, pp.367 and 520.
112. K. Subrahmanyam has expressed similar views in 'They Fought for Freedom Too' *Times of India.* May 9, 2005, New Delhi, p.14.
113. Durga Das. *India from Curzon to Nehru and After.* Rupa & Co, 2001, New Delhi, p. 261.
114. Durga Das. *India from Curzon to Nehru and after.* Rupa & Co. 2001, New Delhi, p. 215.
115. M.J. Akbar. *Nehru: The making of India.* March 2003 impression,Roli Books, New Delhi, p. 358.
116. Lawrence James. *Raj: The Making and Unmaking of British India.* 2001 reprint, 1998 edition; Abacus, London, p. 611.
117. Lawrence James. *Raj: The Making and Unmaking of British India.* 2001 reprint,1998 edition; Abacus, London, p. 611.
118. Larry Collins and Dominique Lapierre. *Freedom at Midnight.* Vikas 1976, New Delhi, p. 120.
119. Larry Collins and Dominique Lapierre. *Freedom at Midnight.*Vikas 1976, New Delhi, p.105.
120. Larry Collins and Dominique Lapierre. *Freedom at Midnight.* Vikas 1976, New Delhi, p. 71.
121. Durga Das. *India from Curzon to Nehru and After.* Rupa & Co.2001.New Delhi. p. 238.
122. Durga Das. *India from Curzon to Nehru and After* Rupa & Co, New Delhi, p. 240.
123. Larry Collins and Dominique Lapierre. *Freedom at Midnight.* Vikas 1976, New Delhi. p.125.
124. Lawrence James. *Raj: The Making and Unmaking of British India.* 2001 reprint,1998 edition; Abacus, London, p. 611.
125. Shashi Tharoor. *Nehru, the Invention of India.* Arcade Publishing, 2003. New York, p. 201.

126. F.Wheen. *Tom Driberg: His life and Indiscretions.* 1990, p. 211.
127. Lawrence James. *Raj: The Making and Unmaking of British India.* 2001 reprint,1998 edition; Abacus, London, p. 606.
128. Larry Collins and Dominique Lapierre. *Freedom at Midnight.* Vikas 1976, New Delhi, p. 111.
129. Larry Collins and Dominique Lapierre. *Freedom at Midnight.*Vikas 1976, New Delhi, p .469.
130. Durga Das. *India from Curzon to Nehru and After* Rupa & Co.2001, New Delhi, p. 383.
131. Lawrence James. *Raj: The Making and Unmaking of British India.* 2001 reprint, 1998 edition; Abacus, London, p. 615.
132. Lawrence James. *The Rise and Fall of the British Empire.* 1998, Abacus, London, p. 551.
133. Larry Collins and Dominique Lapierre. *Freedom at Midnight.* Vikas 1976, New Delhi, p. 93.
134. Durga Das. *India from Curzon to Nehru and After.* Rupa & Co, 2001, New Delhi, p. 244.
135. Brian Lapping. *End of Empire.* 1985, New York, p. 87.
136. Lawrence James. *Raj: The Making and Unmaking of British India.* 2001 reprint, 1998 edition; Abacus, London, p. 636.
137. Lawrence James. Raj: The Making and Unmaking of British India. 2001 reprint, 1998 edition; Abacus, London, p. 624.
138. Lawrence James. *Raj- The Making and Unmaking of British India.* 2001 reprint, 1998 edition; Abacus, London, p. 637.
139. Roberts. *Eminent Churchillians*, pp. 129 to 132.
140. Lawrence James. *The Rise and Fall of the British Empire.* 1998, Abacus, London, p. 551.
141. Durga Das. *India from Curzon to Nehru and after.* Rupa & Co.2001,New Delhi. p.262.
142. 'Constituent Assembly Debates', Vol-I July 22, 1947.

143. 'Constituent Assembly Debates', Vol-VI August 25, 1948.
144. 'Constituent Assembly debates' Vol-XI, November 26, 1949.
145. Durga Das. *India from Curzon to Nehru and After.* Rupa & Co, 2001,New Delhi, p. 279.
146. Durga Das. *India from Curzon to Nehru and After.* Rupa & Co, 2001.New Delhi, p. 274.
147. M.J.Akbar. *Nehru: The Making of India.* Roli Books, 2002, New Delhi, p. 415.
148. M.J.Akbar. *Nehru: The Making of India.* Roli Books, 2002, New Delhi, p. 580.
149. Shashi Tharoor. *Nehru: The Invention of India.* ArcadePublishing.2003.New York, p. 4.
150. M.J.Akbar. *Nehru: The Making of India.* Roli Books, 2002, New Delhi, p. 580.
151. A.L.Basham. *The Wonder that was India.* Rupa & Co, 2002, New Delhi, p. 372.
152. Durga Das. *India from Curzon to Nehru and After.* Rupa & Co.2001, New Delhi, p. 331.
153. Durga Das. *India from Curzon to Nehru and After.* Rupa & Co, 2001, New Delhi, p. 333.
154. M.J. Akbar. *Nehru: The making of India.* March 2003 impression. Roli Books, New Delhi, p. 580.
155. Shashi Tharoor. *Nehru, the invention of India.* Arcade Publishing, 2003, New York, p. 161.
156. Durga Das. *India from Curzon to Nehru and After.* Rupa & Co, 2001, New Delhi, p. 330.
157. Durga Das. *India from Curzon to Nehru and After.* Rupa & Co, 2001, New Delhi, p. 331.
158. Durga Das. *India from Curzon to Nehru and After* Rupa & Co, 2001, New Delhi, p. 329.
159. 'Constituent Assembly Debates' Vol.-XII, January 24, 1950.
160. BBC World Service Press release. December 20, 2002.
161. *Times of India* (New Delhi) – December22, 2002, p. 16.

162. BBC Weekly World Service Programme, 'Wright Round the World' 1.06 pm GMT.December 21, 2002.
163. Christopher Hibbert. *The Great Mutiny, India 1857.* Penguin Books-1980, p. 215.
164. Brian Lapping. *End of Empire.* St. Martins Press, 1985, New York, p. 27.
165. (i) Lawrence James. *Raj: The Making and Unmaking of British India,* 2001 reprint, 1998 edition; Abacus, London, p. 34.
(ii) Colonel Sir Charles Wilson. *Lord Clive.* Macmillan and Co. Ltd.London 1919, p. 94.
(iii) V.D.Mahajan. *Modern Indian History.* 2000, New Delhi, p. 29.
166. Brian Lapping. *End of Empire.* St. Martins Press, 1985, New York, p. 72.
167. Milind Prabhakar Sabnees. Ed. *Vande Mataram.* (Hindi translation by M.G. Tapaswi), Prabhat Prakashan, 2003, New Delhi, p. 45.
168. Milind Prabhakar Sabnees. Ed. *Vande Mataram.* (Hindi translation by M.G. Tapaswi), Prabhat Prakashan, 2003, New Delhi, p . 101.
169. Milind Prabhakar Sabnees. Ed. *Vande Mataram.* (Hindi translation by M.G. Tapaswi), Prabhat Prakashan, 2003, New Delhi, p. 111.
170. Milind Prabhakar Sabnees. Ed. *Vande Mataram.* (Hindi translation by M.G. Tapaswi) Prabhat Prakashan, 2003, New Delhi, pp. 77.
171. Milind Prabhakar Sabnees. Ed. *Vande Mataram.* (Hindi translation by M.G. Tapaswi) Prabhat Prakashan, 2003, New Delhi, p. 44.
172. Rabindranath Tagore. *Gitabitan.* (Bengali) Visva-Bharati. Kolkata, P. 249.
173. *Encyclopaedia Britannica.*2006.http:/www. britannica. com/ed/article-9054048.
174. British Broadcasting Corporation: www. bbc. co. uk / history/scotishhistory.

Index

C

L

M